BEING UNCLE CHARLIE

BEING

UNCLE CHARLIE

A LIFE UNDERCOVER WITH KILLERS, KINGPINS, BIKERS AND DRUGLORDS

BOB DEASY
WITH MARK EBNER

VINTAGE CANADA

VINTAGE CANADA EDITION, 2014

Copyright © 2013 Double D Productions and Mark Ebner

Published in Canada by Vintage Canada, a division of Penguin Random House Canada Limited, in 2014. Originally published in hardcover in Canada by Random House Canada, a division of Penguin Random House Canada Limited, in 2013. Distributed by Penguin Random House Canada Limited, Toronto.

Vintage Canada with colophon is a registered trademark.

www.penguinrandomhouse.ca

Library and Archives Canada Cataloguing in Publication

Deasy, Bob
Being uncle Charlie : a life undercover with killers, kingpins, bikers and druglords / Bob Deasy, with Mark Ebner.

ISBN 978-0-345-81283-4
eBook ISBN 978-0-345-81284-1

1. Deasy, Bob. 2. Police—Ontario—Biography. 3. Undercover operations—Canada. 4. Organized crime—Canada. 5. Organized crime investigation—Canada. 6. Ontario Provincial Police—Biography. I. Ebner, Mark C II. Title.

HV7911.D43A3 2014   363.2092   C2013-901529-9

Cover and text design by Jennifer Lum

All images courtesy Bob Deasy

Printed and bound in the United States of America

4 6 8 9 7 5 3

VINTAGE CANADA

Penguin
Random
House

For my father

CONTENTS

INTRODUCTION

We were sailing along an unpaved road in a rented Chevy pickup, a cloud of dust visible on the horizon and an easy target for anyone who could see us coming.

We were headed for an isolated farmhouse on the outskirts of Perth, about halfway between Ottawa and Kingston. It was the private clubhouse of the Ottawa chapter of the Outlaws Motorcycle Club, a legendary bikers' redoubt that civilians rarely got inside, a place where an undercover cop with his cover blown almost certainly wouldn't make it out alive.

It was 1989 and I was in the middle of working Project Encore out of the Kingston unit of the Ontario Provincial Police's Drug Enforcement Section. Encore was a mid- to high-level drug dealer target project that seeped into a lot of dark corners, including the Outlaws. Billy Scarf, president of the Ottawa chapter, was high on our list of people who were long overdue for an encounter with law enforcement. So there I was, trying to insinuate myself into Billy's sordid world.

Beginning in the late '70s the Hells Angels began rolling over Satan's Choice, Satan's Angels, the Popeyes, the Para-Dice Riders, the Rock Machine and lots of smaller puppet clubs in their bid to dominate Canada's one-percenter outlaw motorcycle scene, destroying everything in their path and assimilating the survivors into their barbarian horde. This HA practice worked well in Quebec and Vancouver, but in Ontario they ran up against an immovable object in the form of the Outlaws, who had the backing of the Italian mafia throughout the province. By the late '80s things were at an impasse, and the Outlaws believed themselves untouchable.

Billy Scarf had no idea who I was—he had guys he paid just to ignore people like me—so first we had to get on his radar. I had an agent who said he could guarantee me entry. An agent is generally a low-level player in the criminal hierarchy whose presence serves to vouch for the undercover officer, at least for purposes of introduction. Like a journalist's sources or a salesman's leads, these characters invariably come with their own sketchy agenda and veiled opportunism, which may or may not be apparent until you read the court records. In this case the agent knew Scarf from years gone by and had agreed to broker an introduction.

I sent the agent in alone first with my cellphone, under the guise of a social visit to Scarf. While the agent was in there

I called him from a pay phone in Perth and laid into him, berating him about a deal gone wrong and screaming that I needed my coke. I knew that at that volume, Scarf could hear every word I said. This ploy accomplished two things: it clearly put me in charge, letting Scarf know I was someone worthy of respect, and it made him curious what kind of maniac would try to force a deal when there were bikers involved. Scarf took the bait. The agent drove back to the town and got me, and the two of us returned to the clubhouse. If I got in it would mark the first time a police officer had walked through that door. And if I didn't—well, best not to think about that.

I parked by the entrance to the sturdy lodge-like structure and took mental note of exactly how much exposure I was carrying. I never carried a gun, and besides, they'd have just taken it from me at the door anyway. Usually I travelled with a cover team—a highly trained, heavily armed backup squad that spots for me in any tight corner and that I would trust my life to on a regular basis. But here we were prisoners of the surrounding geography: there was nothing but open fields and oppressive sky for miles in every direction, with a single straight dirt road leading on and off the property. If something unexpected went down, it would take them half an hour to reach us—not good odds when you're going up against predators with poor impulse control. And so my cover man, Basil Gavin, was waiting back in Perth by the phone like an expectant father, and I was on my own.

A monster of a guy frisked us just inside the door. The single long room featured a bar along one wall and a meeting table in the centre, like something that Vikings would eat off. Chained underneath it was a completely hairless Doberman, like Cerberus guarding the Gates of Hell, missing nothing. The walls had been fortified with oak beams and patched with brick in places and were decorated with biker porn, Harley swag, a paper target from a shooting range. A small room in back was cordoned off with a curtain of glass beads, and a staircase led to a second floor, forming a cramped cubbyhole beneath it with a coffee machine and two or three working police scanners. Above the scanners I saw something that made my blood run cold: Scarf had a list of all six of the members of the Kingston drug unit, and five of them showed their name, make of car and licence plate number. All of them were buddies of mine. It was only because I was new to the region that number six was blank—just waiting for my name to be filled in.

It was early yet, but Outlaws were trickling in, and Scarf seemed to be in an expansive mood. Either that or he was fucking with us. And when guys like that set out to have some fun it almost never ends well. Sitting to my left was a big guy named Skeeter, a hulking bruiser with a waist-length beard. Scarf said to me—a little too casually for my taste, "Before we get started, would you mind giving Skeeter here your keys? The cops don't know your car, and we don't like to draw attention to ourselves." I could have said no, but this would not have gone over well. I flashed him a reassuring smile and dumped my key ring in Skeeter's giant hand. In a heartbeat Skeeter unbolted the back door and was gone.

When he returned, he was carrying a large packet that had obviously been buried outside. He set it on the table in front of Scarf, who opened it and poured the contents through a strainer into a green saucer, then started carving it up into lines. Up to this point in my career I had never had to do drugs in the line of duty. Scarf did a line and pushed the saucer off to his right. When it got around to me there was one line left. Trying to be as nonchalant as I could, I passed it on to Scarf. He stared at it a second longer than he had to.

"Excellent—more for me!" he said, and snorted it right up.

The agent went over to the fridge and grabbed two beers for us. As Billy resumed doling out lines, I noticed a big surly biker—hell, they were all big and surly—across the table staring at me.

"You sure about this, Billy?" he asked, not taking his eyes off me.

"What?" asked Scarf, mercifully slow on the uptake.

"Hey, look, there's no problem," I said, starting in on my patter.

"I'm not fucking talking to you, man—I'm talking to him!"

Everyone at the table drew a sharp breath and held it. "We've never seen this guy before," he said to Scarf. "We don't know him from Adam."

For the first time that night Scarf took a long, careful look at me. I watched as his pupils spun down into dots, each second now the length of five. Roulette numbers seemed to flicker behind his eyes.

"Yeah," he said. "I guess you're right."

CHAPTER 1

GARAGE MAHAL

I'm out in the garage.

Well, it looks like a garage from the outside, anyway. But other than the partly assembled late-model stock car in the corner, it's more like a rundown living room: mismatched carpet, a well-skewered dartboard, a couple of fridges full of Molson Canadian and a white fabric couch scuffed the colour of dirty ice. The house is on an isolated street in the heart of central Ontario countryside. The garage is what civilians would call a man cave, and it might even be the ultimate one, but you won't hear a term like that here. To me it looks as if the house got tilted and only the good stuff wound up here.

On the wall is a 14-point deer's head smoking a cigarette. A framed pic of a sneering Johnny Cash flipping the bird at the camera. An old photo of my late father is beside that. (Dad would've been honoured by a place alongside the Man in Black—the single-finger salute, not so much.) Presiding over it all is a full-size poster of the Flyers' legendary '70s goalie Bernie Parent with the words: "Only God saves more."

The back wall above the wooden work bench has shelves to the ceiling shared by racing trophies, hockey trophies and enough hard liquor to indefinitely sustain a modest pub.

A permanent string of Christmas lights glows overhead. And floor to ceiling, covering any available wall space, are hundreds of mementos and artifacts from my twenty years as an undercover cop—UC, or Uncle Charlie colloquially—interspersed with St. Paddy's Day memorabilia from Chicago to Clonakilty.

It's no museum. If the lights are on, so is the music. Some early U2 to pull Ireland a bit closer. Some Tragically Hip as a nod to Kingston, the hometown. Some White Stripes to bleed the ears.

Come Friday night, you'll find a brotherhood of current and ex-cops of all ages and experience. Crusty old fuckers who've forgotten more about the job than most pencil-pushers will ever know. Young Turks just burning to make their mark, keen to take the torch from the legends they stand among. All of them ready to hear the next great story. Or better yet, tell it.

What started out as a mechanic's wet dream when I moved here with my family a few years ago has become a natural extension of the safe house.

For the undercover cop, as I had been for nearly two decades, the safe house is the ultimate sanctuary. It is many things to many brothers who lead many lives. It's the shelter from danger, a place to seek solace and a lifeline to your allies. It's a place to prepare to face the shit. And a place to decompress after it. A place to get colossally intoxicated. A place to detox. A home away from home. A home instead of home.

And it's a place to be yourself. Or at least to try and figure out what the fuck that even means.

If you've lived to be my age you've earned something like this: a private domain where you're the king of all you survey—or at least a jurisdiction, no matter how small, where you get to call the shots.

The lads dubbed it the Garage Mahal.

For the rest, I don't need to go rummaging through old boxes and file folders. I don't have to dig up buried memories or try to summon stories that should be lost to time. This stuff hasn't gone away. Vivid scenes flash through my brain at the most random moments, especially when I should be immersed in something else. I can be taking my son to hockey practice, and suddenly I'll think, Holy shit, my boy is playing the sport I love! How is it that I'm still here to see it? I should've been dead a hundred times over.

That's what the Garage Mahal is for. The stories we tell here stay in sharp focus. The guys telling the stories had them etched into their memories in the heat of combat. Whether the events we chew over happened a long time ago or more recently, all of them feel like today. My career had its share of wild triumphs and epic failures, billboard-size wins and gut-shattering losses, and all of them happened under assumed identities. But make no mistake—from the painstakingly created persona to the hastily invented lie told to save his ass—all those fictional identities were me, and they've all come to take up residence in my head, full-time lodgers on permanent disability.

And I never once thought, How will I come out the other side? If I was thinking at all, it was, How can I get even deeper?

Watch enough TV and you'll gain an appreciation for the scientific method: forensic pathology, DNA profiling, deductive reasoning and laboratory rigour, all employed by an army of interchangeable specialists utilizing the stuff of daily life—stray hairs, clothing fibres, cigarette ash and bodily fluids—to infiltrate and neutralize the criminal element like a virus. It's fascinating stuff—hell, I watch it too. But talk to a cop who's been undercover in any capacity, and he can top that from a standing start: your day can easily begin in a strategy session at the safe house, have you bear-hugging a biker psychopath by lunch, convincing him you're willing to kill for him, and still be home for dinner in time to hear all about school, t-ball and who's coming to the birthday party on Saturday.

Bad guys get taken down by good police work—feet on the ground, eyes on the prize. I wasn't the first cop to go undercover, and I'm certainly not the last. But I've seen things—done things—that many cops will rarely experience. Getting inside, close enough to the killers, the kingpins and criminal masterminds who seldom extend their trust beyond their line of sight, typically takes time and patience. It always takes nerve. But in that telling moment when you know you've locked in to the heart of someone whose very existence hinges on trust, there's no accomplishment quite so exhilarating.

When I was living the life, I could have walked up to you and convinced you that I was your long-lost brother. And you would've believed it. Because *I* believed it. I come from a long line of storytellers. We're Irish. We know how to hold a room with a story. When I'm one-on-one with some bad character, the room's got an audience of one—and if my story holds, it's going to rock his world. If it doesn't, it will rock mine.

I've spent over half of my five decades inside law enforcement, most of those undercover with the OPP, often in conjunction with its national counterpart, the Royal Canadian Mounted Police. I have completed successful undercover drug operations against the Russian mafia, the Italian mafia and biker gangs, three of what are referred to as the Five Food Groups (the other two are First Nations Warrior Societies and Asian triads). I was also one of the youngest-ever detective inspectors ever commissioned in the OPP.

I remember this seasoned undercover cop who would always say to us, "Go home, UC, go home." You want to make the day even better? Shut it down. Go home.

But you never really shut down. Not because booze isn't the answer. It is, usually. On a rare holiday in England I remember going out for pints with my two uncles who were living and working in East London—tough men in a tough pub in the middle of one of the dodgiest areas in the city. As they necked back their pints of Guinness, I was instinctively taking in the room. When my uncle Pather— who, once famously (albeit foolishly) stood up to the Krays, London's notorious twin homicidal gangsters—asked me what I was looking at, I told him, in his own local, what kind of trouble was about to go down. He didn't believe me—until the fight I had anticipated actually broke out moments later.

True home became the Garage Mahal. Surrounded by brothers who knew what I'd endured in the course of a day meant that I could talk about anything, or not talk about it at all. Most of all, being at the Garage Mahal means you've made it through another day.

Even this old couch has earned its place here. It used to reside at the OPP headquarters in downtown Toronto, and I sat on it for the first time the day I nailed my interview for the OPP drug unit. I'd be in that room and on that couch many times after that day. Some years later, when Bob Rae and the NDP came into power in Ontario, they decided to close the OPP HQ at that prime location, in favour of a new facility in Orillia. The old furniture from HQ was used to fill the temporary offices that would remain in Toronto, which is how it ended up with me at Toronto Drugs. And then at some point it migrated to my cottage, where it stayed for years. When we ended up selling the property the ad read, "Contents included (excluding couch)." If the OPP ever demands it back, subjecting it to a black light would probably be a good idea.

I grew up second-generation Irish in Kingston, not far from the New York border. My mom and dad came over on the boat from Ireland, but work was scarce, and as soon as she had me, my mother took me back to her native Cork. We waited for my father to carve out a beachhead, and when he signed on as a plant man for Imperial Oil, we set sail again for the New World. Every summer I went back to Ireland to stay with my grandparents, but only one of my parents could afford to go at a time, so they took turns. (In those days young children travelled free.)

A startling presence at six feet six inches tall, Pat Deasy was the kind of stern Catholic patriarch and disciplinarian who inadvertently withheld even the simplest emotions from my brother and sister and me. He had no shortage of passion for sports, though. He'd never seen a game of hockey until he came to Canada, but he set out to learn it so he could coach my house league team. (I played everything from centre to wing to defence from the time I could stand on ice.) Since he was so tall as a kid—in his Grade 5 class photo it looks like there are two teachers—he was treated with an implicit respect he kind of grew into. We first settled in Brockville, and then when the Imperial Oil plant closed we moved down the 401 to Kingston. I grew up poor but proud.

The old country never left us: Irish music was a constant soundtrack to my early life, and my father always had a bottle of Jameson within arm's reach for medicinal purposes. When my mom—who was all of five feet tall and a teetotaller—had had enough of it, he confined his drinking to the truck or out with his pals. He was a pillar to lean on for a great many people, but he had a fuse as short as an oil-lamp wick, and when you poured whisky on it, it was just like kerosene. He had a hard-and-fast, black-and-white sense of right and wrong, and when you crossed that line, he'd go off on you like a cannon. That went double for his kids. Since I was the oldest, I became the first line of defence for my mother and brother and sister when he was in his cups, partly by my own design. I figured I could take it better than they could, so I got wheeled around quite a bit. At one point my mother was all set to pack her bags and take the younger kids with her, leaving me behind to break it to the old man, but luckily it never got to that. Soon afterwards he stopped drinking for good.

From the time I was out of diapers, whatever my dad was driving, I got behind the wheel of. He drove a tank truck, and at the docks he'd have to unload the Great Lakes Oil freighters. The job took exactly twenty-four hours, and when the ships would come in, my mother would send me down to meet Dad in the Kingston dry docks and he'd have me for the whole time. I can see now it was just to get me out of my mother's hair.

Everything bad that happened in Kingston happened in the Kingston dry docks. It was the home turf of the criminal element and the epicentre of everything reprehensible about humanity. This became my playground. The oil refinery plant was some distance from where the freighters came in, and from an early age I would invent reasons why I should drive a forklift or a pickup truck up the hill to the refinery or warehouse. Eventually, I wore my dad down, and from the age of eight or nine, he let me drive up and down the hill. I was in heaven; that's all I wanted to do in life.

The absolute high point of my week was Friday night, when I got to drive Dad's stock car up onto the trailer for his weekly race. I still race stock cars with my own son in tow and have a shelf full of trophies to show for it, but that's where the impulse comes from.

The Kingston area has nine federal prisons, assorted psychiatric hospitals—even a prison museum—many of them built overlooking Lake Ontario, some of the most desirable real estate in the province. During the Kingston Penitentiary Riot in 1971, when I was nine years old, six prison guards were held hostage for four days before being released unharmed. The city was in a state of lockdown—there was no traffic; the only sounds were the helicopters overhead, making everything spooky and otherworldly —and my father and I walked over to get a closer look. We could see the inmates from where we stood, when they would come out onto the roof and unfurl bedsheets on which they had written their demands. A few years later, when I was in Grade 7, my friend's dad, who was a Kingston plainclothes detective, was shot and killed while serving a search warrant. I remember the teacher and principal coming into the gymnasium where we ate lunch and taking my friend out. I could hear him crying in the hallway outside. It was my first experience with death, and my dad sat down with me that night and we talked about it. So it's possible that my earliest memories of police and policing are inextricably linked with my father as well. When he died in 2000, I vowed to get a tattoo in his honour, and when I gave up undercover work in 2002 (where any distinguishing mark can be a death sentence), I had the Deasy family coat of arms tattooed on my right upper arm in black, white and green; it's faded now, perhaps, but is a permanent badge I wear with the pride of the blood that runs beneath it.

The one part of my childhood that I've consciously adopted into my professional life, though, comes from the time when my father was running the local St. Vincent de Paul Society in his spare time on a volunteer basis. St. Vincent de Paul is a charity run by the Catholic Church, similar to Goodwill, with a warehouse where people can donate clothes or furniture, as well as a food bank. We grew up squarely blue collar and frequently hand to mouth, so it was easy to identify with the people who frequented these services, and I acquired a sense of empathy in me that frequently came in handy in the more benevolent aspects of police work. It seemed as if everyone in Kingston had our home phone number, and many nights I accompanied my dad on some errand of mercy to the poor part of town. Along the way I got a good education in human behaviour and learned that much of what we might tend to label negligence or delinquency from a distance is no more than good people dealing with bad situations in unfortunate ways.

I also got a good sense of when people were in desperate straits, and when they were running some scam. With the many half-way houses and inmates' families struggling to survive, we had our work cut out for us. In retrospect, it was the best training for undercover work I can imagine.

I was the first in my family ever to attend university. On the Carleton campus in Ottawa, I discovered a number of things about myself in quick succession: it was my first real introduction to class divisions; though I had grown up without much expendable income, that never really seemed to make a difference back in the neighbourhood. But the main thing I found out was that I could fit in anywhere. I also became aware that from a very early age I could talk to anybody. I never had to consider social rules or unspoken codes to fit in—I was always at home wherever I went, and people naturally confided in me. I was at home with the stoners—I knew how to snap the bottom off a two-litre bottle of Pepsi to smoke hash. And I was literally at home with the jocks—I lived in a house with a bunch of guys who were later on the Canadian weightlifting team in the 1984 Olympics, and who were disqualified and sent home from Los Angeles when they were found guilty of doping.

I studied criminology, and planned to go to law school. During my last year, I wrote a paper on "The Subculture of the Police," and my prof arranged for me to ride along on a shift with Ottawa uniformed police. When they worked, I worked. It was almost like a full-time job. The variety of calls we answered meant that no two shifts were the same. It was both gripping and draining. For me, an otherwise contented university student, this sudden and unfiltered exposure to the world of crime and police work was nothing short of fascinating. I spent a year studying the insular world of police work—the tradition and social reinforcement that make law enforcement an integral part of society, yet somehow apart from it, circumscribed by a society and code of behaviour all its own. The public service, the problem-solving, the band-of-brothers loyalty and the unexpected spikes of danger and adrenaline—I found all of it immensely appealing. The calls as they come in are all the same—whether a cat stuck in a tree or a multiple homicide—and yet the variety of human experience makes each one different. And the variety didn't just come from the side of the calls; from what I observed, there were as many ways to do the job as there were jobs to be done. As my pal and undercover man's man Smitty has put it, "It's like a library of human suffering, and you're the librarian."

During my time in university I played safety for the football team, and when I graduated, I entertained the thought of playing for the Ottawa Rough Riders, the local franchise of the CFL. As glamorous as that may sound, the job paid $21,000, which I would have had to subsidize by driving a taxi to survive. Looking to head off a life of disappointment and physical pain, my dad finagled me a legacy offer from Imperial Oil that would have started me at decent money. Around the same time, the cops I had been doing ride-alongs with invited me out for a beer and basically told me that I was born to do what they did: I had the street smarts, the people skills, the ability to think on my feet and an intangible quality that put people at ease. They encouraged me to apply. What I couldn't have known is that the timing perfectly coincided with a shift in policy to integrate more college-educated candidates into the law enforcement system. Whether the order came from on high or not, I wound up being just what they were looking for.

Although I wouldn't know it until the opportunity presented itself, it's just what I was looking for as well. My dad drove me to the interview. At the end of three hours they hired me. Within a couple of weeks I was at the OPP academy in Brampton, the first step in a year-long probationary position.

And everyone thought I was insane.

CHAPTER 2

THE DURATION POST

My life as a police officer began in the middle of nowhere.

At some point in your OPP career you are required to do a duration posting, typically a northern detachment, ranging from one to five years. Most cops choose to do this right at the start rather than uproot their life down the road. My detachment was in the town of Geraldton, just off the Trans-Canada Highway, three hundred kilometres northeast of Thunder Bay, with nothing but forest in between.

Carved out of the woods, Geraldton—population one thousand back then—was probably a kilometre and a half long between the city limit signs, situated near several First Nations reserves. The detachment also policed the Aroland settlement to the north near Nakina and Ogoki Post, a fly-in reserve two hundred kilometres due north. When I got there in 1984, I was one of twenty uniformed OPP constables assigned to cover roughly forty thousand square kilometres of isolated terrain across the centre of the Canadian Shield. When a new cop is assigned to a duration post, especially right out of police college, the entire town knows you're coming. They know you don't want to be there, and they know you're not staying.

In addition to being a conspicuous outsider, I had to deal with the harsh realities of my new situation. They roll up the streets at 10 p.m.; the first week I called home wondering aloud to my mother what I'd just done with my life. To make matters worse, she told me that Peel Regional Police near Toronto had called and offered me a job just days after I'd accepted the OPP position. I had to call them back and tell them I was going to stick it out up there in the Great White North.

"Good for you, kid," the Peel cop said to me.

There were several motels in Geraldton. I bivouacked in one of them for the first two weeks—pressboard walls and no sound insulation make you feel as if you're living on display. What no one had bothered to explain to me was that in addition to being the site for probationary assignments like mine, Geraldton was also known to be a penal detachment (which sounds painful, and probably is, but not in the way you're thinking). This is where OPP officers who might have screwed up elsewhere can get assigned.

The police station was located in one of the only brick houses in town, a family home with the living room and dining room cleared of furniture save for a conference room table and chairs and given over to police business; the detachment commander and his family had lived there at one time. A second bathroom had been repurposed as a jail cell.

Most local housing was clapboard or prefab houses or trailers. My first house was a tarpaper shack, part of a leftover mining camp, where my only friend was a one-channel black-and-white television with rabbit ears. Gold fever had overtaken these environs in the 1930s, more than a quarter-century after the Klondike Gold Rush had given out and its crazed denizens had moved on. As a result there were still active gold mines in Geraldton up to 1970; it's kind of where the dream came to die. The hardscrabble life demanded by mining meant that some of the toughest, meanest, most disagreeable people in the world ended up in Geraldton. Later on, when I needed a cover story working undercover in the Far North, I used everything the old-time prospectors had taught me to mask my frequent disappearances.

The town was largely populated by French-speaking bush workers—men who worked hard and played harder. A fleet of school buses fanned out across town at three-thirty or four every morning to take the cutters out into the bush. These were the people who routinely worked eighteen-hour days and then hit the bars with plenty of cash and the desire to blow off steam as quickly and efficiently as they could.

There were three bars: the Gold Nugget, the Silver Nugget and the Geraldton Hotel. A local airstrip existed to accommodate, among others, the American tourists and weekend hunters, as well as the firefighting crews for the giant water-bombers that were stationed at the Ministry of Natural Resources base on Wild Goose Lake, all of which added to the mix. Most drug activity emanated from Thunder Bay.

The first year of a two-year duration assignment is measured out in baby steps: a month in, and you can drive the patrol car by yourself on the day shift; after three months, you can take it out alone at night. You could go days without seeing another soul on the Trans-Canada. If a strange car wandered off the highway and showed up in my town, I'd know about it within the hour.

It doesn't take much imagination to see that if you're in uniformed police work you're liable to see people at their worst: nobody calls the cops when they're having a good day. As a result, a lot of cops look at their constituency as the dregs of humanity. This sort of attitude will not buoy your spirits over the long haul, and the repeat calls to the same houses where the same residents face the same domestic challenges can certainly make you jaded. But that's true everywhere.

As a cop you can drive around with your windows up and do your patrol—run the clock down, apprehend suspects and school the miscreants as best you can, but sometimes you have to park your car, walk a beat and interact with the locals. People are information, information is knowledge and knowledge is power: the more you know, the better you can do your job. In very little time in Geraldton I gained a reputation for anticipating a problem on the strength of my recon, and for being able to quell a lot of disturbances before they escalated to handcuffs and nightsticks. Maybe it was all those night patrols with my dad, parachuting into people's lives in times of crisis and trying to patch things through to the clarifying light of day. I figured out how to get a situation resolved before it ever reached the point of no return. This approach gave me a degree of respect among the locals, as well as a kind of rapport I wouldn't have had access to otherwise. Later on, when I'd catch the participants in a quiet, sober moment behind the school or outside the liquor store, we could talk out some of these ongoing tensions, or they'd volunteer information about other problems or crimes. People may be part good or part bad, but they generally aspire to the good.

Take something as simple as groceries. Since we were so far off the beaten path, a head of lettuce might be a quarter in Thunder Bay and ten times that in Geraldton, so if any of us in the detachment were going to Thunder Bay, we'd head out in the cruiser with a giant list of supplies for local residents and make the 640-kilometre round trip in a day. We'd take turns being Grocery Santa.

It seemed that every shift I worked there would be a fatal moose accident out on the highway. A couple of times a year the local moose population is attracted there: in summer insect season they're driven mad by the swarms of mosquitoes and blackflies and make their way out to the open road, where there's a cool breeze to offer them momentary relief; in winter, if it's snowing and the highways have been salted, snowplows have pushed all the snow into the ditches, where a 680-kilogram moose can stand and lick the salt, which is like moose heroin. By then he has so much venom in him from the blackfly bites that he easily becomes extremely agitated. So when the Grey Goose regional bus comes through, the moose takes it personally.

The first time I dealt with such a collision I got a statement from the driver that he was looking directly into the moose's eyeballs when he rammed the bus, came through the windshield and pinned him in the front seat. When I got there the moose was alive, and there were deep grooves in the highway for twenty or thirty metres, where he had dug in his hooves. We had to chainsaw off the antlers to get him out of the bus. The moose just gave his head a shake and trotted back toward the treeline.

Most of the problems we dealt with stemmed from alcohol, due to the widespread addiction among the local population. When they couldn't get alcohol, they drank "blue," the street name for windshield-wiper fluid. When they couldn't get blue, they huffed gasoline or drank mouthwash. There was no creative threshold to getting high. I was horrified by some of the things I saw there. There were eight adjacent units in a small townhouse complex that the government had built at one end of town as low-cost First Nations housing. Not too long after the ribbon-cutting ceremony we got a call to that address, and the place was destroyed inside: doors had been torn off the cabinets, carpets ripped out, windows smashed, holes made through the walls into the next unit. It was just as if a bomb had gone off inside.

Sometimes you try to find the humour in a bad situation. Geraldton also had a two-storey mental health facility that catered to a dozen patients and outpatients at any given time. One of them was someone we called the Crazy Lady on Main Street, because people would call the station and say, "You know that crazy lady on Main Street? Well, she's out on Main Street acting crazy again." One night in the dead of winter, right after a two-metre snowfall, she flagged us down while we were out on patrol. She and her boyfriend, who weighed maybe four hundred pounds and was in a wheelchair, had cashed their welfare cheques and gone out drinking. The bars had closed, and a taxi driver had dropped them at their place on the edge of town, but he couldn't get near the house on account of a snowdrift. The boyfriend could technically walk, but he was too drunk to. She had tried to push him up the walk in the wheelchair, but he had become stuck in the snowdrift, and she was afraid he'd die of exposure. We drove up there in our 4x4 Dodge Ram, and she was right: he was trapped. Applying ingenuity in a crisis, as we're taught at police college, the other constable and I decided that if we could get the 4x4 up there, we could push the wheelchair out of the snowdrift and onto the porch. It being far below zero by then, this seemed like an excellent plan.

I got behind the wheel, and Ray, my partner, guided me carefully up the path. When my bumper met the back of his wheelchair I eased down on the accelerator. I could feel the RPMs rising, but he was not moving, so I leaned on it some more. Suddenly the truck got traction, and in a heartbeat he was out of the chair and on the ground. The crazy lady started shrieking, "You killed him! You ran over him!" Lights were going on up and down the block, and people were coming out of their houses. Seeing an OPP utility vehicle, a wheelchair upside down and a fat guy facedown in the snow, they would be entitled to think whatever they wanted. We tried to haul him back into the chair, but he weighed as much as a moose, and our heads collided, causing us to stagger backward, which just made us start laughing, and we dropped him back in the snow. All this time he was flailing around and bellowing at top volume. If they'd had cellphone cameras a decade earlier he would be the Rodney King of Canada and we'd be—well, probably still in Geraldton, since there's really not a grimmer place they could send us. At any rate, we finally got him back into the chair, up onto the porch and inside his house before the pitchforks and torches came out. That's a story that could have ended considerably worse.

My time in Geraldton taught me that there's a great deal of latent resentment on the part of Native people against whites—or at least white cops—and it manifests itself in mostly passive-aggressive ways.

Trying to have a basic conversation can be like pulling teeth, and it makes the cops I know mental, which is probably its intention. The subtext seems to be "This is my land, and there's nothing you can tell me that I need to know."

At one point we had a train derailment on the CNCP rail line, which follows the Trans-Canada Highway east to west across the country. It occurred on native land, in the northern stretch of my sixteen hectares of purview. Any-where else in North America and there would be helicopters, video feeds and a thousand rescue workers assembled from every regional authority.

One of the derailed cars had lost its cargo: faux leather jackets—pleather—destined for some dollar store in western Canada. The normal procedure was to secure the area, manage any casualties, prevent pilfering and determine cause, in that order. Since no one was hurt, I went into town to talk to witnesses to determine what might have happened. Every single person I encountered was wearing a size forty-four pleather bomber jacket—seven-year-old kids with the arms hanging down, old women bent over double. And no one had any idea what had happened—in fact, they seemed sur-prised there had been a train wreck at all.

Geraldton was where I first encountered the emotional toll of human drama.

Ninety percent of what I did there was handle simple domestic disturbances in which alcohol played a decisive part. It was not uncommon to see people in their twenties and thirties who appeared twice their age due to alcohol and the elements. One of my friends, a long-time resident who became a bit of a mentor to me in First Nations ways, was named John Agamaway. I had written him so many tickets for being drunk in a public place, which merited a $13 fine, that I just wrote "John" on the top and tucked the ticket in his pocket. After thirty unpaid tickets, a judge would issue a Warrant of Committal, which the accused could voluntarily retire by serving four days in jail. Since no one ever paid the $13 fine, I waited until the week of Christmas and then went out and rounded up the year's offenders and took them to the jail down in Thunder Bay. Everybody got three meals a day in a heated cell, they ate a big Christmas dinner and they got to dry out for a week before the start of the new year. It was generally appreciated.

Of all the characters, John was my favourite. I would make a big deal of swearing him in as my deputy and drive him all over the territory where everyone could see him in his official capacity, and where he could give me the lowdown on everything happening in town. For an hour or so he would be sober and able to impart his considerable wisdom.

John was staying in a dirt-floor shack along the railway tracks a mile outside town with another friend of his and a woman named Mary. For all three, drinking was their only enterprise. Mary wasn't with either of the men technically but would allow them to take turns climbing on and off her if it kept the peace and got everybody back to drinking sooner. Generally she was passed out when this took place. Everyone seemed contented with this arrangement.

One day John's friend walked the distance into town to the police station and said, "You better come. I think I just killed John."

Both men had decided they wanted to have a ride with Mary at the same time, and being the larger of the two John prevailed. For reasons he couldn't really explain later, the friend took an axe and buried it in John's chest. When we got to their shack Mary was sitting against one wall with no idea what had happened, and John was lying there with an axe in his chest. He was only in his mid-forties, but the pathologist later told me that John's heavy drinking had turned his insides to jelly. I had been around violence before, both personally and professionally, but this was my first experience with death by misadventure. At twenty-three I could only interpret it as tragedy and was all the sadder because of it.

During my two years in Geraldton, since I was single and there was nothing else to do, I spent a lot of my spare time compiling drug intelligence on the town—what little drug activity there was, mostly weed, hash and coke. Keeping tabs on the scene turned out to have some use.

In July 1973, following a significant increase in illegal drug use around the province, the OPP had created the Drug Enforcement Section (DES) of its Special Investigative Branch, tasking thirty specialized officers—cumulatively known as the Flying Squad—to form joint forces units dedicated to drug-related law enforcement, formerly the sole jurisdiction of the RCMP. In 1979, the DES opened its six regional drug units across Ontario and separated all administrative operations from the RCMP, henceforth co-operating on a project-by-project basis. In 1988, when public pressure demanded more focused public strategy against drug encroachment provincially, the decade-old DES drug units were perfectly placed to serve as the tip of the spear. Here was a ready-made, rambling configuration of drug warriors, the elite thirty-man army of undercover operatives of the six regional drug divisions. Members were hand-picked and nominated from within, creating an efficient, streamlined, tight-knit organization of self-starters, all motivated and extremely resourceful.

Whenever an undercover operation from one of the six units ventured over onto our turf in Geraldton, they would call up our detachment and ask if there was an intelligence officer who could send them a package to get them started. Since I knew all the players in our area, I invariably became that guy—whether they needed a breakdown on a potential target or someone to toss a car on Main Street. At one point four guys came up from Thunder Bay Drugs to conduct an undercover project and requested local assistance. I met with them—they looked like members of the Grateful Dead—and after hearing them out I was hooked. They let me know they appreciated my help, and when there was an opening in their unit they'd put in a request for me to come and join them. I applied for a transfer, and two and a half years after I'd come to Geraldton it was all set.

I was on my way to the Thunder Bay drug unit.

CHAPTER 3

BABY NARC

The guys I'd teed up in Geraldton did everything but lay out the red carpet for me to get to Thunder Bay. Whenever a drug team spotted a decent prospect, which apparently didn't come along all that often, they'd send word up the chain of command that they had a live one, and you would get a request to put in a formal application for transfer. The guys who sponsor you are sticking their necks out, so their word carries some weight.

When the request came through, my boss, a staunch uniform guy with a drawerful of hard-earned wisdom, gave me a flat no. "If you go into the drug unit, son, you'll ruin your life," he told me. "You're a good policeman. Stay being a good policeman. Do not get involved with the drug unit." From his point of view everything about the drug-warrior lifestyle was antithetical to traditional law enforcement: they worked when they wanted, dressed like gypsies, roamed the land like vampires, associated with the worst elements of society and flouted the basic principle of command and control. Specialized drug units were still relatively new, and the lifers who bled blue thought their members were all deranged. Transfer request denied; end of story. Except that eventually the detachment commander went on vacation, leaving my corporal in charge, a guy named Dave Wall, who eventually made it to chief superintendent, which is two spots away from commissioner. He is widely respected today and, if I may say so, an excellent judge of character. I stopped by his office late one Friday and said, "Would you mind signing this for me?"

He looked at the paper and then back at me—sizing me up, but also weighing my circumstances against what he knew of his immediate supervisor.

"Yeah, I'd be glad to, Bob," he said.

Three weeks later I got a call from drug-unit headquarters in Toronto inviting me down for an interview with the superintendent.

I drove the twenty hours from Geraldton to downtown Toronto and got there around noon. It was like any police precinct or newspaper office in a movie: everyone running around, phones ringing, a beehive of activity. People stopped by on their way somewhere else and asked me who I was—"I'm the new guy"—but no one seemed to have any idea what to do with me, and I ended up waiting most of the afternoon.

Finally, at the end of the day, as the secretaries were

packing up to leave, I got word that the superintendent—a white-haired Irishman named Webb Craig—was ready to see me. He couldn't actually have been that old, but his authoritative demeanour probably added thirty years to a first impression. At his invitation I sank into a white couch—the same couch that would one day grace the Garage Mahal. He seemed distracted but of the old school, by the book, and he asked me three or four questions, which I answered confidently. Almost apologetically he added, "You know, son, you may be exposed to some things here that you've probably never seen before. I don't know how prepared you'll be to handle these types of things."

I told him, "Sir, I've seen the strippers in Geraldton; I can handle anything you can throw at me."

He laughed and said, "You're hired." The whole thing seemed pro forma; I could have phoned it in. They basically just wanted to get a look at me and make sure I wasn't some idiot who was going to get killed the first week and make them look bad.

Craig took me down to Mr. K's, a pub on Victoria Street, where everyone I'd seen bustling around me throughout the day came by and offered congratulations. Craig gave me a canned speech about how much he hated problems and ended it with "Okay, kid—no shenanigans." A fine Irish word, shenanigans.

I squared my life away in Geraldton, moved to Thunder Bay, then flew to Toronto, where I was issued an '86 powder-blue Ford T-Bird and $1,000 in cash and directions to a safe house in Barrie, where a drug project was already under way. I was to watch and observe one of the UCs for two weeks as a sort of makeshift orientation, and then I would be on my way to Thunder Bay to start my new life. I would still be a constable, at the same salary, but rank is really only good for putting on your business card, which doesn't come up a lot in undercover work.

Whenever municipalities or police departments around the province believe they have a drug problem, they contact the provincial authority, which assigns the case to one of its six regional drug units. The local cops are too well known, and their resources too constrained, to successfully penetrate beneath the superficial street layer and make their way up the drug chain. They need specialized outsiders to do that for them. It's up to the local constabulary to work up a dossier and identify key players and prospective targets so the undercover team can hit the ground running—the kind of work I did up in Geraldton. Local authorities also arrange a safe house for us—a nondescript rental in an unassuming area just outside of town where the undercover team can live and work without drawing undue attention to itself. On the outside the safe house looks completely generic, but inside it's been transformed into a mobile police station: in my time, the kitchen table was stacked high with field notes and exhibits; there was a bulletin board with photos of the targets—a "who's who in the zoo"; fax machines buzzed constantly and there was usually a single beige Touch-Tone phone that everyone used. The bedrooms are off limits—they're where the UC dumps everything in his personal life that he doesn't have time to deal with.

When I knocked on the door of the nondescript suburban house in Barrie, an obviously unbalanced person exploded from behind it and barked, "What the fuck do you want?" I turned and was headed back to the car, mumbling something about Smitty and vague directions, when this guy shouted, "Look what they sent us—a pretty boy!" While I was still standing there on the front porch, he said, "Did they give you any money? Quick— hand it over." Before I quite knew what was happening, he had fleeced me of my roll and my car keys. Only then did he invite me inside.

This was my first introduction to Smitty, and by extension, to the Flying Squad, the storied band of run-and-gun undercover DES drug agents known for their subversion of authority and their lax views on official protocol. Over the years Smitty has become a friend, a mentor, a life coach and a personal hero. He's also one of the funniest guys I've ever met. (He once tracked a suspect to the town of Beaverlodge in the wilds of Alberta. They met at the actual Beaver Lodge, which had a painting of a giant beaver on one wall. The guy said, "You want to get your picture taken with the beaver? Everybody does." Smitty told him, "Hell no, man. That's what broke up my first marriage.") He'd probably merit his own book, except for the fact that Canada has no statute of limitations on his brand of hijinks.

Inside the safe house it looked as if I'd interrupted a meeting of the bikers' book club: feral monsters in leather and chains lounged around on ratty furniture, looking up from their newspapers or their knitting to see what new prey had just wandered into their fright-night fairy tale. These, I was to learn, were members of our illustrious cover team.

When you're undercover your cover team is your lifeline. We always have a handful of guys who are permanently assigned to us who watch our backs, run our reconnaissance, carry our firepower and manage our money. Since everything we do is a special project, our funding comes in a lump sum for everything—rent, groceries, bar tabs, drug buys. If you're in the middle of bringing down a criminal empire you don't want to have your phone shut off because you forgot to pay the bill. A lot of them are sweethearts—Basil Gavin, my cover man on the Project Encore case, was a lovely soul with a picture-perfect family—but most of the time, their appearance does four-fifths of the heavy lifting for them. They look like genuinely evil, rotten miscreants. Your cover man is like a mother hen, if she rode a Harley and had a giant Komodo dragon tattooed on her chest.

Our cover men were always there with us—a rotating crew with names like Caper, Zit and Joey Montana—not their real names. These guys looked like the devil's henchmen, especially if you were a brush-scrubbed recruit right out of boot camp who stumbled into their upcountry platoon of heartbreakers and wife-takers. From almost the first moment I got there, these primitives sat around the main room, poking at me and debating among themselves what they could do with me. [You guys do know that I can hear you, right?] I was just grateful they didn't boil me down for soup. They went home only to sleep, and when we were in the middle of twenty-hour days their wives would bring dinner over because they knew we wouldn't stop working long enough to eat. Of course, after we had rolled up the project and left town, these guys would stay behind and reap the glory. But they still went above and beyond. Forget that they kept us alive: one of them would come through and tell everybody to throw their rancid, motorcycle-oil-soaked clothes in a green garbage sack and take them home and wash them. We were all cut from the same cloth.

Because of its proximity to Toronto, the safe house ended up being an all-purpose meeting place or safe haven for personnel on their way from one place to another, to reconnoitre or to just let off steam. Kind of the first of the Garage Mahals. This was in the days before computers, cellphones or text messages, when, if someone needed to have a fruitful talk with you, he'd get in his car and come see you. So I wound up meeting everyone in the drug enforcement community pretty quickly. I was also the first of the newbies they sent down for the Smitty treatment—the first of many. It was Narc 101. He used to complain that he was running a daycare, and eventually they sent down some grizzled drug veteran about to make supervisor (whom we nicknamed the Forehead) to translate Smitty's makeshift life lessons into an offical curriculum. But Smitty took a special liking to me—even if he made sure I was the last one to know it. His instructions to me at first were fairly simple: "You can buy drugs; you can't sell drugs." Other than that I was on my own.

It was decided early on that they would take me to one of the uptown bars where the rest of them couldn't get past the doorman and drop me off curbside. No sense having a college preppie and ex–glee club member in their midst and not get some mileage out of it. They settled on the Brookdale, the house bar for rich college girls with Daddy's credit card and the frat boys who chased them for a living. Luckily the Beautiful People demographic was one I had some hands-on experience with. And Beautiful People Smitty and his backwoods clan were not.

My cover guys drove me and waited outside in case I ran into any trouble. I skated past the bouncer without a hassle and soon had the room sorted as to who was the drug crowd and who was not. To acquire some cover in plain sight, I started talking to another guy there—about girls, sports, whatever. He was a white guy about my age, blond, decent-looking. After a while he asked me if I wanted to smoke a joint, so we went out to the parking lot and continued our conversation. He had an "oiler"—hash oil or honey oil spread on a rolling paper and rolled up with a cigarette, which gives it a slightly golden tinge. After half of it he said, "The rest is yours," and went back inside. I snuffed out the joint, put it in my pocket and was thrilled beyond measure that I'd scored my first buy right out of the gate.

When we got back to the safe house Smitty and his cover man, Johnny Miller, were already in for the evening. There was a pile of dope on the table that they were weighing with scales and bagging as evidence.

"How'd it go?" Smitty asked without looking up.

"I made my first buy tonight," I said. This was kind of unheard of. The others stopped what they were doing.

"Well, let's see it," said Smitty.

I pulled out the roach and handed it to him. There are very strict protocols on how to handle evidence: you're supposed to state the exact time you hand the evidence over, the way a physician would note the time of death, and then log it and seal it in a plastic bag. Instead, he flicked it across the room.

"Are you fucking kidding me?" he said. "Go back tomorrow, see the guy and buy some dope from him. And don't come home with this!"

Very soon I started producing results. It seemed I had a knack: the storytelling gifts of my father and grandfather turned out to be a sizable inheritance after all. And all those late-night runs we'd taken to minister to people at their most desperate had drummed into me a sense of empathy that allowed me to read strangers as easily as the phone book. Criminals are criminals for a reason, and if the reason is that they're tired of going without, or they get hypnotized by the shiny bits on the Christmas tree or the presents that ought to be underneath it, I didn't need sensitivity training to explain that part to me. I never lost my academic eye—the ability to see criminals as specimens, pinned and wriggling in a pattern of their own design—and I would come to meticulously document and archive every stage of a case with scholarly zeal.

Unlike a lot of guys in this line of work I had a long fuse. I could hold my anger in check far past the point where others were washed downstream by their emotions. If I needed to, I could wait a long time to settle a score. A lot of guys would leather up and grow their hair to their ass and think that to beat the monster they had to be the monster. Come a showdown you'd see their eyes roll back and they'd go mental, raise the hair on the back of your neck—all muscle and intimidation, jazzed up with just enough crazy to make even the stone killers think twice. But that wasn't me. All I had to do was be the monster's best friend.

Smitty used to say, "There are two kinds of horses: workhorses and show horses. And you, my friend, are a show horse." While pretty boys like me waltzed in and sipped our wine spritzers, the mules like him were doing the real work down in the mines. He never stopped busting my chops. But my one insight early on was that the entire undercover business was all about talking. You'd talk your way into a situation, and if your career was going to have any longevity you'd talk your way back out of it. Smitty called us peoplesmiths, as opposed to blacksmiths, gunsmiths or wordsmiths. That was our trade. It didn't matter how you looked or dressed or if you behaved in a certain way. If you had the part down too perfectly, you just became a copy once removed from the real deal. The trick was to get the real you into the mix, get them to accept you as what you said you were, and then start firing on all cylinders. It was improv at gunpoint: suddenly drop character or go up on a line, and a bad review would come as decisively as Tony Soprano's final fade to black. That can put you in the moment like a motherfucker.

Once I made that leap they could put me anywhere they wanted. The chic nightspots and rarefied haunts of the rich and privileged became part of the territory just because I didn't look like one of the cave people from *The Time Machine*. Smitty is one of the most gifted undercover cops I've ever seen, and in the twenty years I did UC work I saw his exploits become the stuff of legend. But two weeks into the job I could already do something he couldn't. Without any of them quite anticipating it, suddenly a whole hemisphere of drug connections and clientele opened up to them. I became the missing piece, a counterbalance to Smitty's loose cannon and the sewers he was expert at running in. That was heady stuff for a twenty-three-year-old.

The first undercover job you try to run is on the people who recruited you. They're watching you like the hawk watches the field mouse, from a thousand metres away with laser vision. If you can get over on them, you can get over on anybody. They are predators and they're looking for themselves in you. When they know you're one of them they'll stroke you and coddle you and raise you as their own. They are also loath to let you go.

By the end of my two-week probationary period the sergeant in Thunder Bay was calling every day, asking when I was coming back. I was always conveniently "on assignment," and Smitty kept talking him in circles. Every morning the cover guys had to file a report on the previous day's activities, and they would stress that it would be premature to send me to Thunder Bay. I was in too deep. Meanwhile, they were a man short in Thunder Bay, and the bosses there were getting hysterical. Finally, Smitty phoned Toronto and explained apologetically that I was the linchpin in a whole new part of the operation. He was sorry for the inconvenience, but it would probably be best if this new recruit remained in their charge for the next little while, at least until they could wrap up the current phase of investigation. Thunder Bay Drugs would have to wait.

I came for a two-week crash course and wound up staying for a year.

The operation we were running in Barrie was known as Project Tornado. It took its name from a tornado in the '70s that had devastated the city, coming off Lake Ontario and forming just west of the 400 through a natural trough of some of the lushest, most fertile farmland in Canada. This was a ground-up operation, which meant we weren't setting out to bring down a kingpin. We built the case up from the street urchins, shit-rats, drug dealers on the corner, leather coats and lounge lizards until we got to the mid- to upper-level full-time dealers, most of whom were connected to sources in Toronto. Lots of our re-ups—re-buys of drugs—were done in Toronto, so we'd jump in a car and drive the hundred kilometres due south into the city. These jobs were all done on the fly in parking lots outside train stations, Tim Hortons or highway rest stops, usually with guys in Trans-Ams with leather jackets, coiffed hair and shiny cowboy boots. All the top-end guys were bikers from the Para-Dice Riders and the Loners, both of which eventually got folded into the Hells Angels. They ran things out of a peeler bar called Crossovers where all the strippers were bikers' girlfriends. (Everyone called the place Bendovers.) After everything went down, the cover team's phones rang off the hook with patches (full-member bikers) looking to give somebody up and make a deal. I don't care who you are, nobody wants to spend his life in prison playing euchre for hand jobs. Over seventy went into lockup.

Probably my most harrowing experience on that tour of duty—the first time I saw Smitty suit up and take the field, and the experience that best illustrates the difference between us—was when he took me to the Simcoe Hotel, which was ground zero in town on undesirables and the street-level drug trade. There was a rooming house upstairs, and you could get anything you wanted on the premises, as long as you had the balls to take it or could handle the consequences. It was the *Star Wars* cantina for criminal species, or *Deadwood* with Harleys and hogs instead of horses and wagons. And for the year and a half he was there Smitty owned the place.

Walking into the hotel bar, I did what I did in every bar the first time out: buy a beer, then put a quarter on the pool table. Smitty went off to find whoever he needed to find, when out of nowhere this big freakazoid took a sudden dislike to me and put me up against a wall with a buck knife at my stomach. Big knife. Smitty was holding court, and I tried to make eye contact with him before this guy reduced me to giblets. Smitty saw me, but from where he was sitting, it looked as if the freak and I were just exchanging words. Some version of this always happens with new guys—the alpha dogs need to sort out the pecking order, and it's easier to just get it over with. After a minute or so Smitty casually made his way over to us. When he saw the knife he started yelling: "Hey, Shit for Brains, what the hell are you doing? You hurt him and I'll never hear the end of it! He's my wife's cousin. I ain't sleeping in the garage for six months just because you got some problem. You got a beef, you take it up with me—I'll get you whatever you need from him." An endless stream of patter followed until the guy lowered his knife. Smitty bought him a beer at the bar. The worst part was that I had to stick around and shoot pool when all I wanted to do was get in my car and drive home.

Smitty walked me through it later, as if we were watching game films the day after: get him to look at you, break his attention, divert him. Be his new best friend. Keep him from concentrating on what you're saying to him, because once he starts paying attention, that's when you're likely to get all jammed up. Smitty used to say he could go to the twentieth anniversary of the Space Shuttle pilots and hold his own for ten minutes. Minute eleven, they'd see through him like cellophane, but he knew for ten minutes that he had them, so he could manoeuvre his way out of anything.

What set Smitty and me apart from everybody else operationally was that at the end of the day—unlike the cover team, our visitors from Toronto or whatever wandering vets or renegades assisted us in our campaigns—when everyone else folded his tent, drove back home, played with his kids, watched the game on TV and deep-dived his wife, Smitty and I were still there. We were assigned to work ten days on and four days off, during which we were expected to decompress, return to our regular lives and ground ourselves in something more substantial than the thrill of the next takedown. But since neither of us had a real home to go to, Smitty and I were stuck there, staring at each other's ugly mugs. To compound matters, we couldn't go out socially—to a bar, a restaurant, a garage sale or anywhere else—because if we were out we were working. We'd have to put on a uniform and a game face, which would defeat the whole purpose. We'd be without our cover team, or else they'd be working. Left to our own devices we could watch old movies, drink heavily, play board games or work up a wicked crossword habit. But eventually a kind of cabin fever or spiritual malaise would set in, which is when most of the problems arose.

This uncomfortable state of affairs led to the exercise of something called Policy Change, a reaction to sufficient negligence on the part of officers as to require some prohibition of actions or adjustment to formal protocol: "From this day forward, such-and-such will no longer be tolerated." That thing you did? We're not going to do that anymore.

There was a lot of Policy Change in those early years: "Officers will not advance money in a drug buy." Sorry, but if you don't front the money, there's no deal. "Officers will not use sufficient force to break a suspect's arm." That one had nothing to do with me, but once you try to update a code of behaviour to keep up with suspects' allegations, it's going to get messy. "I sold him five hundred hits of acid, but he also had intercourse with me, and, you know, I think I'm pregnant with his baby." Oh, sorry—is that sort of thing frowned upon?

The introduction of new technology—new toys—also resulted in Policy Change. Years later, when Smitty and I were working together in Kingston, we were issued the first two portable cellphones on the force. They were huge things—heavy, each with its own battery pack. And like any kids on Christmas morning, we played with these things constantly.

"Hey, guess where I am?"

"I give up."

"I'm in the parking lot!"

We took separate cars on a two-hour drive from Kingston to Cornwall just so we could spend the time there and back on our cellphones. This was at early adopter rates. At the end of the month our phone bill was something like $800.

Policy Change: "No officers shall use official cellphones for extended private conversations."

Another Policy Change that we were responsible for was "Be careful whom you use to accomplish your ends." We arrived at a bar where an alleged seller hung out, only to discover that his wife worked there as a waitress. We chatted her up, and she invited us by the house the next day to buy a gram of coke. When we got there the husband refused to have anything to do with us, and in fact denied that he sold coke at all. She told him, "Oh, don't be such an asshole. They just want a little bit." She essentially nagged him into selling us half an ounce.

This was close to the end of the project, so four days later, after the takedown, we arrived back at the police station and the desk sergeant said, "There's a girl in the lobby who looks like a raccoon, says you guys are responsible for almost getting her killed." It was the guy's wife, and once word went out that busts were going down, he had tuned her up. She could barely speak because her jaw was wired shut. I understand that probably doesn't look good from the departmental perspective, but we don't force people to break the law. All I could fall back on was the *Animal House* defence: "Hey, you fucked up. You trusted us."

One Policy Change would have precluded all these adventures with a single stroke of the pen: I made undercover in two years; now you need at least five years minimum in uniform before you're eligible for undercover in a drug unit. But the thing that really got us in serious trouble was when we were issued brand-new firearms. That year the OPP changed firearms manufacturers, and to get out of the office, one of their middle managers took a drive up from Toronto. When we got back to the safe house, our visitor had left on the coffee table two small plastic cases that looked like black cigar boxes, with our names on them on yellow stickies. Inside we found two regulation Heckler & Koch P7 9 mm semi-automatic handguns noted for their portability and ease of deployment, and Smitty and I would be among the first police officers in Ontario to carry them. We were ordered to turn in our old .38 snub-nosed revolvers.

I'm not really a gun person. I never carried mine and rarely even knew where it was. The joke was that if I got in a jam while driving around I'd slam on the brakes and hope my gun would slide out from under the front seat. I underwent weapons training and am qualified to carry in the field, but usually I can't be bothered.

A lot of UCs go unarmed. We've got cover teams whose business it is to defend us, and there are a lot fewer accidental shootings in high-pressure situations as a result. If I need it I've got access to the best-trained Tactical Response Unit (TRU) team in North America. And just speaking personally, I've never seen a criminal deploy a weapon in the field. The only thing I've ever shot in the line of duty is a moose. The mob guys are like us: they've got professionals to carry guns for them. And the bikers and other cowboys who run the dope trade usually don't need guns to make their case. Those guys *are* weapons.

A weapon is like a pet you don't want to have to take care of. You can lock it up at home, but then the first time you take it out in public it's just as likely to bite someone. I've taken plenty of beatings in the line of duty, but it's pretty rare to get wasted in a bathroom over a gram of blow.

Smitty, on the other hand, is a gun fanatic—a collector and a massive hobbyist. After he opened his cigar box and unpacked his replacement weapon he field-stripped and reassembled it in fifteen seconds—*ch-ch-ch-ch-ch-ch*. I left mine in the box. He yelled at me to come on and bounded down the four steps to the cinder-block basement where the washer and dryer were.

There was a crawl space running the perimeter of the basement, and Smitty had me take one of those children's plastic Halloween jack-o'-lanterns that the family before us had left behind and place it at the far end of the space. As soon as I'd cleared the entrance, a tremendous boom sounded, and the target flew all over hell.

Smitty argued that it was only responsible for us to adequately test our weapons before their deployment in the field. And since we were bivouacked there incognito, precluding our full use of the grounds and environs, we were forced to conduct such tests in an enclosed space. This reasoning possessed a certain logic. (Alcohol may have been a factor.) He handed his gun to me, and I aimed and squeezed off a round. The pumpkin danced like Baryshnikov. Holy fuck—this was awesome. I ran back up and got my weapon, and we spent the next several hours blasting makeshift targets in this concrete box and dodging the ricochets. It's a wonder neither of us were killed.

Smitty and I had a code word we always used as a signal—a kind of "Beam me up, Scottie" to cue the takedown team or as a safe word for any situation we needed to bail out of in a hurry. This came in especially handy in a rip, which is where we ripped off the drugs in a drug buy and arrested the participants, usually at the last stage of a year-long project.

After we had made the buy, as soon as we uttered the word "Florida"—since we were always wearing a wire—the ninja team right outside was supposed to sweep through the door and roll up the bad guys. These takedown teams know what they're doing, and they're pretty serious about their jobs, so you want to get out of their way as soon as they spring into action.

At the end of Project Tornado, Smitty and I picked up a target outside his house, rumoured to be a member of the Outlaws motorcycle club. We had him sitting between us in a GMC pickup truck, and we were driving all the hell over the county trying to do this deal. There had been a renegotiation and a re-renegotiation, all par for the course; I was wearing a wire and we were dragging a full surveillance team behind us everywhere we went. They like you to move once, and not far, but tonight we were like Pac-Men, gobbling up the scenery. Every two minutes it was "Stop here"; "Stop there"; "I need smokes"—the dude was edgier than a cat with a sparkler in his ass. We finally settled on a price, and he directed us outside of town and had us pull over at an abandoned gas station. By now the sun was going down.

Smitty said, "We're meeting your guy here?"

He said, "Oh no, you don't understand—I can't take you guys there. He'd kill me if I showed up with anybody else. You have to give me the money and I'll go and get it."

There are a few cardinal rules in a drug deal, and one of them is don't advance the money because you'll inevitably get burned and it will all be on tape. But we knew the whole town was going down anyway as soon as we got over this hump. At that point we could taste it. Smitty said, "Okay, fine. Give him the money."

The guy said, "Yeah, but I need your truck."

Say what?

"I don't have any wheels, man. I've got to go get the stuff."

Smitty just shook his head, and we slid out of the cab and watched him disappear into the night in our GMC pickup. We knew the spin team was out there in the darkness somewhere watching us, as we stood on a concrete slab beside an abandoned gas station with our asses in the wind.

Smitty said, "I don't care what you just heard; this was your idea."

"I had no part of this," I said directly into the mic. "*None* of this."

The truck had only one headlight, and twenty minutes later we saw it approaching on the highway. The spin team never lost sight of it, but they had no way of contacting us, so as far as we knew he had sold the truck at Honest John's and was on his way to Mexico with a backpack full of government money. By the time he returned we were a little loopy. We climbed back in the cab, the guy between us, noticeably without any drugs on him.

"So where is it?" Smitty asked.

"He doesn't have it yet; he's waiting for it to arrive," the guy said. And the money? "He's still got the money. And I'll need your truck again to go pick it up. I thought you guys might be getting nervous, so I came back out here."

Us? Nervous? No way, bro. The ninjas were already melting back into the treeline, since now they knew where the drugs were, although we didn't know that. It was clearly time for the takedown—my first—and because things had already gotten so screwy Smitty couldn't resist making it a party. He launched into an epic tirade about the project and the whole past year of our lives—recounting the deal before us as well as our other actions and overall existential reflections: well, that was quite a year. I can't believe we did this and got away with it. Remember when we did that? Remember when that happened? What about that guy—wasn't he a piece of work? It almost had an elegiac feeling about it, and the guy must have thought we were about to cap him—as if this was some weird gangster shit or *Pulp Fiction* thing we did right before we sent our pigeons flying.

"Where would you like to go this time of year?" Smitty asked me.

"Me, I'm thinking maybe . . . Connecticut."

"Pennsylvania. New Mexico . . ." We must have named all fifty states with the exception of Florida. It was all we could do to keep from cracking up. Every time it came back around, you could feel the ninja team out there pulsating in anticipation. Finally, Smitty leaned forward to where he could see me and said, "You had enough of this yet? We done?" I nodded, just as Smitty unholstered the Beretta they had insisted he wear and put it to the side of the guy's head, chambering a round.

"I'm going to fucking kill you if you so much as move your hands a quarter of an inch," he told the target.

The guy was certain we were going to murder him for the dope and leave him in a shallow grave, a feast for the raccoons and meadow mice. He started sobbing and begging us not to kill him.

I told Smitty, "I think he just soiled himself. I've got to drive this truck tomorrow."

Smitty said, "Where we going, Scully? *Florida!*" and the surrounding area exploded. Cars came roaring up the highway two abreast from both directions and slid into the gravel lot. Black-clad ninjas raced across the open field. We yelled for them to go after the drugs, but they were already all over it.

"The money *and* the truck?" our boss asked us when he saw us. "What are you, fucking high?" The next day the rest of the network fell like dominoes.

Fourteen months after my arrival, Project Tornado was successfully brought to a close, and I made my way to Thunder Bay to take up the life that had been deferred for over a year. Smitty went to the Kingston drug unit. There had been periodic complaints from the neighbours in Barrie that something wasn't quite right about our set-up at the safe house, although we were routinely given a wide berth. After we had departed, a sergeant in the Toronto drug unit found a single spent 9 mm shell casing in the basement, and all hell broke loose. I had been down on my hands and knees wriggling into every tight corner of our impromptu shooting range, but missing that two cents' worth of used brass was threatening to send what seemed a promising career ass over elbows. I was a month into my first solo project in Dryden when word came down from on high that a biblical-calibre storm was coming. A major investigation was launched, since virtually every cop in the DES had been through the house at one time or another. They threatened to seize everyone's firearms and run ballistics tests. I told Smitty, "There's no reason to put everyone else through that. Let's just say we did it."

Smitty took a deep breath. "Look, kid, I'm long in the tooth and I've got a history," he said. "I'll take the rap. They'll have to weigh however mad they are against my whole career. You, they just might send back to uniform."

I said, "I'd rather let the chips fall where they may. What kind of police am I if I buckle at the first sign of pressure?"

So the next morning I phoned my boss in Toronto and said, "You don't need to investigate any further. It was us."

"No, it's wasn't," he said. "We know it was Smitty and you're covering for him." Whatever I said, they had made up their minds and I couldn't get them off the dime. But since I'd confessed, they had no choice. "Policy Change: there will be no discharging of firearms inside a safe house."

The incident instantly entered OPP police lore. I had been scheduled for a transfer to a southern unit, where all the high-level projects emanate, just as soon as I'd completed my first solo run in Thunder Bay. And Smitty was set to take the test for a promotion. As our penance, Smitty wouldn't get to take the test, and I wasn't coming south.

I embarked on a year of service in every one-horse town across the northern arc of Canada, from Kenora to Cochrane.

I called it the Northern Tour. In hindsight I saw it was the best thing that could have happened to me, because rather than go from being the weak link of a crackerjack drug unit, to the hot dog who suddenly had to prove himself, I was able to put all that training I received into practice on my own, far from the withering eye of the official bureaucracy, and to figure out undercover work so that it worked for me—without a bunch of legends around to make me look good by association or catch me when I fell.

I packed my long handles for one more run at the Great White North.

At the end of eighteen months I had missed two close friends' weddings and a slew of family commitments. I went home to see my parents once, unannounced, and at first they didn't recognize me. The only thing I owned when I left uniform was three green garbage bags full of clothes and a black Trans-Am, my pride and joy, which I had left in short-term parking at the Thunder Bay airport before my detour to Barrie via Toronto and the powder-blue T-Bird. When I finally went back to get it I owed more in parking tickets than the car was worth. It was as if the old me had been suspended in time and a new me had materialized out of thin air to take its place. Now I could be whatever I wanted—likeable, popular, heroic, badass. I was a blank canvas, and my eyes were open for the first time.

CHAPTER 4

THE FLYING SQUAD

During my early years undercover a couple of things happened that brought about sweeping changes in police culture. One I've already mentioned—the emphasis on college graduates, which created a smarter pool of candidates for sought-after positions and resulted in a generation of UCs with a higher-education background. The second was Benji Hayward.

Benji Hayward was a fourteen-year-old Toronto high school student who attended a Pink Floyd concert at Toronto's Exhibition Stadium on May 13, 1988. Hayward and a friend took two hits apiece of blotter acid and either snorted coke or smoked crack at the concert before getting separated in the massive crush on the way out. The friend was stopped by police later that night wandering in a drug-induced fog, but Hayward apparently vanished—a fact that the Toronto police appeared to take lightly but his parents did not. Unhappy with the official response, Hayward's parents blanketed the vicinity with flyers.

After Hayward's body was discovered four days later floating in Lake Ontario near Coronation Park, it emerged that Toronto police had stopped both boys two months earlier for drug possession but had failed to notify their parents. It also came to light that in the case of the Pink Floyd show, police had deferred all drug deterrence efforts to the concert promoters, who often outsourced concert security to biker gangs suspected of widespread drug dealing. Anyone familiar with the crowd control at Altamont could readily identify this decision as a potential public relations nightmare. Again, a public outcry galvanized the police community and forced them out of their set ways, and the OPP drug unit doubled in size practically overnight.

Just as I was making my bones in the undercover drug world there was a mandate to make drug enforcement part of the national agenda, including a police priority. At the same time there was intense public pressure for these glowering, autocratic fiefdoms within the constabulary universe to drop their individual guard and get along, which was like taking a dozen trained pit bulls and leaving them in the backyard to play. Even if they had wanted to comply, they were mystified as to how.

Enter the OPP Drug Enforcement Section's legendary Flying Squad, the world I emerged into after the Geraldton detachment and my trial by fire in Barrie.

Prior to 1973, all Ontario drug cases were the mandate of the RCMP. The thing that made the Mounties good at combating most crime—a rigid police culture, a reputation for humourlessness, a Dudley Do-Right persona—made them especially terrible at drug crimes. Through no fault of their own, squeaky young RCMP were deployed to Ontario straight out of Depot, the RCMP college in Regina. With little or no street experience they had to try to survive in a self-sustaining drug subculture where they could not have seemed more out of place. It was the same fate that befell the FBI in the U.S. during the '60s and '70s, and it required a similar ground-up solution. (The U.S. Drug Enforcement Agency was formed in 1973.) And so in July 1973, when the OPP joined forces with the RCMP and added an additional thirty officers to its Special Investigative Branch to create the Drug Enforcement Section, the Flying Squad was born. These new operatives had the ability to fly beneath the radar to new locations and covert assignments as circumstances dictated. In 1979, the OPP decided to go it alone, forming six standalone units throughout the province. In 1988, when the operation was greatly expanded, adding three more regional drug units, they welcomed a wave of people like me.

And who were these people? Let's just say there were a plethora of broken moulds when it came to the individuals who were crazy enough to make this particular career choice. One of the OPP's earliest inductees was a guy we called The Pope. He could have the air of a mischievous boy—and more opinions than he was entitled to. One of those guys who came off the assembly line without a reverse gear, so woe to you if you ever got at loggerheads with him. The OPP sent out a blanket telex stating if you're interested in applying for the drug squad, send your name and badge number and they'll contact you if they feel you'd be suitable. He put in his application like a lot of other guys and got called for an interview in downtown Toronto.

When he walked into the conference room, a couple of white starched shirts were waiting for him. One of them said, "Tell us a bit about yourself." And before he even sat down, he answered, "Well, I'm actually a woman." They assumed he was kidding, but he just sat there stone-faced. It so happened that he had an anomaly with his urethra, and during surgery, they were forced to make an incision at the base of his scrotum, so for the time being he wasn't able to urinate standing up, which he dutifully explained to the interviewing officers. He was hired on the spot.

Much later, during the expansion around the time I arrived, there was another guy we called Neutron, on account of he was pretty far out there. He was a uniform cop up in Dryden, and a dead ringer for Billy Bob Thornton. Inspector Bill Burke and a corporal known as Smokin' Joe Lucas were conducting a Northern Tour where anyone who applied got an interview. Neutron walked into the room carrying a spit cup for the lip full of chewing tobacco he was rocking and said to Burke, "Can you hold this for me?" Part of the interview entailed a role-playing scenario, where Lucas was the dealer and Neutron was the UC and buyer, so they could judge the calibre of his banter. So Neutron takes the lead:

NEUTRON: I understand you got some weed for sale. How much you want for it?

LUCAS: $3200 a pound, but I don't really know you, so I'm not comfortable selling it to you.

NEUTRON: Go fuck yourself. That's way too much money. I'm not buying your fucking dope. My price is $2800—take it or fuckin' leave it.

It escalated from there. Finally they were in each other's faces, and Lucas at least was not playing. Inspector Burke had to step in between them to calm the situation down. And then they immediately told Neutron he was hired.

(Come to think of it, they hired me on the spot when I delivered the line "I've seen the strippers in Geraldton—I can handle anything you can throw at me." There's a reason so many Flying Squad alumni are such characters: we tend to hire our own kind.)

The Flying Squad was largely free to build alliances with the rest of Canadian law enforcement and to move porously between its declared borders. For a lot of the old-timers that meant the opposite of good police work. To them we were out there doing what we were doing without any sense of restraint. In their playbook anything unregimented was the province of chaos. Inside our bubble was just the opposite. We dressed the way we wanted, established our own protocol, took the fight to the enemy, lived their life-style, adopted wholesale their Faustian bargain—yet emerged unscathed with their scalps on our belts. We didn't flout the rules because we were somehow above them, or because we were rebels without a care; we knew the rules forward and backward. We circumvented protocol for purposes of efficiency, to gain ground or momentum on criminals who didn't believe in rules and exploited the fact that we did. We were spies behind the lines of the drug war, living by our wits. We didn't bend the law, but a lot of times we did scuff up the bureaucracy.

And we produced results. That's because we had learned from our betters and sought to harbour their tradition through uncertain times. We did what we did for Queen and country but also for the guys who had passed the torch to us, who we came up idealizing and wanting to be like—guys like Dennis McGillis and Terry Hall and Normie Brown and Gordon Montgomery—badasses all, who among them established a good part of Canadian case law. Some of them have had books written about them, and some are known just within a small band of acolytes. Some became our first tier of supervisors, and they understood the realities of the way things worked at the street level—when to lean into an executive order and when to give us room to manoeuvre. We were like a fraternity or a brotherhood, bonded by common goals but also by the sacrifice and shared hardship that had gotten us there. You let these guys down, and you can never be one of them again.

Smitty nicknamed us the Nine-Man Rolodex because after a while, as our stars rose and careers progressed, the same nine people got tapped for all the toughest long-term jobs. There was Normie and Neutron and Pipes. Dino and YaYa and The Kid. Of the guys I'm closest to, in addition to Smitty, there's Scotty, a.k.a. Spanky or Hoagie, whom I met in '87 and who became a full-fledged member in 1990: pockmarked face but good-looking, like a cross between Ray Liotta and Tommy Lee Jones. And there's Robo, who became a GT (Greater Toronto) city cop, where his day-to-day consists more of homicides, turf warfare and your standard urban crime. With his long stringy hair and the aura of menace that surrounds him, Robo most resembles Gregg Allman in his heyday. He could have been one of the world's great used car salesmen. He and Scotty have worked together a lot, and he's become a great friend and confidant to me. He actually owned our safe house in Barrie; he and some other guys bought it as a rental property. My nickname in the group, the one Smitty gave me, was Skully.

Our immediate bosses always knew what we were doing—though sometimes not until after the fact. The major decisions were never made at our level: who to target, where to allocate resources, whether to go to a full-blown takedown or else take what we've got, grab the headlines now, scare a few of the locals straight and move on. Benefit-to-cost ratio, statistical efficiency, declarations of war and terms of surrender—these were all above our pay grade, but given a fixed set of goals we would plan the tactical campaign. These situations were often so fluid, and our actions so dictated by the moment, that there was really no other way to go. We didn't choose the what, but we did decide on the how.

Consequently, our bosses had the hardest job imaginable. We UCs were policemen held to the highest accountability, in a sphere of operations where a great deal of attention was paid to supposedly quaint notions of right and wrong, good and bad, but they were in charge of a platoon's worth of the most extroverted, Type A personality, self-directed, thinking-on-their-feet, scamming bastards you could assemble in a single place. These are guys who, to a man, have deceived the world into believing they are someone else, and who never slip up, under de facto penalty of death. So the really good bosses—the ones cut from the same cloth as we were—you couldn't bullshit them. They would always call your bluff.

The problems started to arise when the accountants back at HQ decided to approach everything from serial rapists to drug projects as stand-alone operations, subject to the market principles and sterile formulas they learned in business school. Now police work was no longer treated as a government service, like electricity or wastewater management, but rather as a series of discrete incidents or agendas, each in competition for shrinking resources and subject to the fanciful demands of teams of armchair generals and their blind, misplaced confidence. Once operations are being run from a spreadsheet, everything gets triaged and cost cutting becomes rampant. The murders that come with a confession or a smoking gun get solved; the ones that require legwork and undue man-hours slowly lose priority, like a leaking zeppelin. And when this impulse runs up against an ongoing undercover effort, with its own momentum and human capital camouflaged as enemy assets, it means they're managing risk from the safety of a cubicle. Which works about as well as robot golf.

How this affects actual policing is that you'll get an adviser who will blow in with his buzzwords and quantitative analysis, schedule your appointments with criminals and druglords for weeks down the line, second-guess your on-going negotiations, saddle you with bureaucratic require-ments, monitor your odometer and phone bill, put you on a ticking clock and line-item veto your requests for phones, pagers and backup. These operations sometimes take years and millions of dollars, and yet they become subject to the fleeting ripples of quarterly reports and managerial infight-ing. Imagine the Normandy invasion run by MBAs. You can have the Medellin Cartel establishing a supply route to your sleepy bedroom community and half a dozen UCs in place waiting for them, and some bean-counter who's never seen a day of combat will call you up and say, "That's a *lot* of money. We're going to have to rethink this."

This mindset is endemic throughout law enforcement, if not everywhere else. It's just that we're literally on the bleeding edge. You can't make rules about something you don't understand. And you can't demand a signature on a receipt for buy money when you're dealing with a guy named Scooter who has filed his teeth down into tiny points.

So as encroaching authority began to dismantle our ability to make decisions in the field, we began to limit their knowl-edge of what decisions needed making. Project plans and daily reports had to become more vague, airier, generically goal oriented, until eventually we could run things the way we wanted. Before you know it you're setting up your own import-export office to back up your cover story because it's easier than asking for help from people who are essentially clueless. Such narrow management style begins to breed a culture of deceit. Undercover work is basically lying for a living anyway; it's the one skill we're already adept at. In classes he led, Smitty would say, "You ever lie to a loved one? Tell your wife a little white lie at four in the morning? Did you go back later and clear that up? Well, then, welcome aboard." Extending that MO to include politicians and upper management was not much of a stretch.

The other impediment we routinely faced was that would-be accord with other police groups, particularly the esteemed Royal Canadian Mounted Police, who had a culture unto themselves—an institutional forced camaraderie that usually gets mangled in practice. We were constantly assigned to combined task forces, with no rules on the books to arbitrate the inevitable disputes. Although every one of us has dear friends in the Mounties, they are very much Canada's police force, with a rule and protocol for everything they will encounter in their day. They have a workforce of something like thirty thousand, but they're just not built to turn on a dime the way we are. If I was undercover with a Russian crime family and my target said, "We're going to Vegas this afternoon," I'd throw some shirts and a toothbrush in a travel bag and head to the airport. My RCMP equivalent would initiate a week of meetings, telexes and executive-level approvals that would leave him ready to travel by the time we got back. The RCMP want us to work with them, but only up to the point that they can control every physical aspect—a constant source of frustration for UCs.

The best description I can give you of a Mountie, better known in my world as a Horseman, is from the TV series *Breaking Bad*. Walter White's bullet-headed brother-in-law Hank Schrader, a U.S. federal Drug Enforcement Administration cop, is a Horseman in everything but name. He shows glimpses of ingenuity, but every piece of information has been handed to him. He doesn't mine it himself, so he's oblivious to its context and often its meaning. He reads a report, and it reminds him of some random bit in a previous report, which he heroically connects. This would be ideal if crime were a crossword puzzle or a mystery novel. He's basically an observer, whether he's doing it from a laptop or a parked car. But I guarantee he'll be around for the photo op when they're writing the newspaper story about it.

We had a joke around the office: Three K-9 units are called to the scene of a drug bust. The Toronto police dog goes into the house first and finds a kilo of cocaine. The OPP dog goes in next and finds two kilos of cocaine and a kilo of heroin. The RCMP dog gets there last, fucks the Toronto dog, fucks the OPP dog and calls a press conference.

The Mounties have a playbook and they stick to it. They keep their sources locked up like a child bride. They freebase the limelight. And they hang together right or wrong, stand by their orders and their errant brothers, regardless of the damage done. Their innate conservatism and stick-in-the-colon stance can make them stand out like a pastor at a porn shoot. I was on stakeout with a Horseman one night who started to testify about his recent religious conversion. People already thought he had two wheels up off the track. I told him, "That shit is like condoms; you keep that in your wallet and don't tell anybody about it." We didn't like him even when we liked him.

The RCMP are incapable of adapting or evolving, so they become the worst thing you can be when dealing with criminals: predictable. They'll cultivate a drug source just so they can buy "gram, gram, kilo"—a gram the first time, another gram on the re-up and then jump to a kilogram. (That would translate to $50, $50 and $5000.) It's their by-the-book policy, and every criminal knows it by heart—they ought to put it on a T-shirt.

I had a bad guy once, on his way to doing serious time, tell me, "Those federal clowns? They're all idiots. The municipal guys? They couldn't find their ass with a sharp stick. But you guys, you always made me nervous. You're sneaky mother-fuckers. I always thought if I'm gonna take it up the ass, it will probably be from you guys. And here I am. My ass is sore, and I'm talking to you." I had another mob guy tell me, "Twice I thought I smelled a fucking rat. I got to get my nose checked."

As Smitty said when he first started sleeping with the female federal officer he's been with for the past twenty years, "Nothing gives me greater pleasure than to fuck the Mounties."

So instead of relying on the liaisons assigned you, you start to circumvent the procedure. You call in favours wherever you can find them. You follow your own guys out into the hinterlands, wherever they land, and they become your sources, a network of like-minded individuals in place to overcome the hurdles that are handed to you. You learn to trust your own for everything, whether it's a place to stay, a hot meal, a phone number, a background check or some real-time corroboration in word or deed. Your guys are a phone call away, and they're always ready to get airborne or in the wind. As far as I can tell, this is unique to the drug unit. The whole undercover thing is like a force field around you. And inside it are some of the smartest cops in the world.

Instead of requesting a surveillance team and waiting for approval from upstairs, I might see if a couple of these guys have some downtime and could come over and sit on a house for me. They're not getting paid, so there are no personnel reports to file. They know the drill, so I don't need to field-train a recruit or fret over liability. There's no interdepartmental paperwork because we're just a couple of guys shooting the shit in a parked car or knocking back a few at the safe house. The next day or two everybody's safely at work. But the thing gets done. And I'm on call to do the same for him. As long as we're cranking out the numbers and putting up the stats—the bodies—it would be nothing for one of them to say, "I bumped into a real tough nut last, and this guy is really giving me a time." We're on the phone to each other every night anyway. We tell each other where we are in our cases, run scenarios by each other, work out our strategies and cover stories. A lot of the time it's easier to solve other people's problems than it is your own—step into their world for an hour or two and move the pieces around until they fit. Before you know it, instead of sitting around some safe house trying not to draw attention to yourself or compromise your own case at some particularly delicate stage, you're in a car with two or three of your buddies, barrelling across the province, getting ready to blow some guy's mind in a bar.

We did this for each other constantly, for as long as I've been a member of the Flying Squad. No UC, no matter how gifted he is, can simulate an entire life indefinitely. After a while, since these things go on for years, the lack of other people in your life starts to be a blaring absence: no women, no family, no friends: you've got a circle drawn around you, and eventually it feels like a target. So some weekends when we were off the clock, half a dozen of us from our far-flung assignments would converge on a comrade in need—Scotty, for example—and roll out to the bar with him. Before, he was a lone wolf who kept an extremely low profile. Now he was the ringleader of a crew of mad dogs who made him the automatic centre of attention wherever he went. We'd get shit-faced, buy rounds for the entire bar, pump endless dollars into the jukebox, dance with the ladies. We were a human tornado, and when we rolled out, the one thing everyone was sure of was that

Scotty was no cop, because they'd just met his whole crew. He was golden; people stood in line to be his friend.

The people who ran the projects, the powers that be, had no idea. Nor would they have handled it well if they did: twelve or thirteen of the most extreme extroverts imaginable, probably stoked to the gills on Jameson or Maker's Mark, on a midnight run to spread psychic mayhem among a bunch of deranged, armed psychopaths. No liability issues there. We did it on occasion for other UCs who asked, like the long-timer who showed up at my safe house door one night and told me, "The last solid food I had was an ice cube," and proceeded to lay out a tale of woe about how he wasn't getting any respect. We did it when dealers were trying to fool with the purity of their product and the UC needed to establish that he knew what was going on and not look like a pushover, or when he needed to show some muscle to move up the buying chain, or when he needed recon on someplace he couldn't walk into because they knew him or it would get back to the wrong people. We thought of these as cameo performances, and the more theatrical the better.

Later on, when Smitty was running a street team in Kingston, serving search warrants as part of a typical city drug unit, Scotty and I would routinely show up and help him kick in doors. It was what we'd do to blow off steam on a Friday or Saturday night, and it was an immense amount of fun. With the exception of my two years in Geraldton, I never really had the experience of being a cop—at least not in an urban setting.

I don't own a uniform, never rode in a police car, went on patrol, responded to a call, got to say "Ten-four" into a radio—at least not as part of a functioning police force.

One time Smitty got an advance prototype of a hydraulic corkscrew-like tool—he was always a bit of a gadget guy—that was supposed to pop the deadbolt off a door. He explained the principle as he screwed it in on a reinforced-steel door on the apartment of a drug dealer, but it wouldn't pop. After a minute the steel door started to warp and bend in toward the inside. We heard a woman's voice on the other side say, "What's happening to my door?" She passed out when she saw us—it's possible she might have been expecting a poltergeist.

When the bosses finally found out that we were recreationally going out on police raids to unwind, they were nearly hysterical. I remember one guy yelling at us, "We've got $100 million tied up in drug ops—you can't be out there kicking in doors!" I can assure you they were less concerned with our safety than they were with their investments.

It's no mystery why we spend our off hours together, or bond over the pressures at the office, since our biggest undercover challenge may actually be our home life. You're out mowing the lawn in your best Jimi Hendrix shitbird Afro, your Amish-Polish beard, your Harley-Davidson wife-beater and chain wallet, and suddenly your wife is yelling at you to take it down a notch before the neighbors call 911. "You don't need to look like Marlon Brando just to cut the grass!" You miss your wife's house party, your kid's school play, the church social, the neighbour's barbecue, christening or graduation, and not only is there no adequate apology to make to your family and friends, but the community looks at you as if you're a sociopath. Any excuse you come up with isn't good enough, nor is your explanation for why you need four different cars in the course of a year, why you're gone for months at a time or look like Shaggy from *Scooby-Doo*. No wonder we're crashing into other people's living rooms for fun. Or why we are all on our second marriages or involved in common-law relationships—with lady cops, no less. There isn't one of us who wouldn't turn down the occasional ill-advised drink, or isn't out somewhere when we ought to be home in bed. Sometimes it's just easier to leave the costume on.

It's that same bond that keeps us from going rogue. Beyond the easy jokes—"You know, we could make a lot of money on this"—I've never been tempted to cross the internal bright line that separates me from the people I'm tasked to pursue. I suspect that's true of most of the guys I'm close to. I may be naive, but for me at least it's never come up. For me, if one of us goes sideways it's far worse than a normal cop falling off the path because the other UCs gave you such power, helped you develop another identity, trusted you with the freedom to make your own decisions—even in the most ethically ambiguous situations. And *then* you went sideways?

Compare that with the DEA, for instance, whose agents sometimes think of Canada as the cute little hat perched on top of America and all of us in Canadian law enforcement as the McKenzie brothers or *The Gang That Couldn't Shoot*

Straight. But America's "war on drugs" is driven by money—police departments that have to justify their budgets, politicians who need it to run on and agents who rarely break a sweat unless there's a price threshold attached. If I were a DEA agent and I wanted a nice car, I'd find a criminal who was driving one, plant a rock in his car and the car's mine. Here we don't have access to seized proceeds of crime. We don't need incentives; we work for a living.

Not to argue that there aren't a lot of ways to go bad: "Shit, tits and tires," as the saying goes. You throw the three of them into a blender, it's gonna come out radioactive. Every UC knows that if you dip into the product—even if forced to in the line of service—it's going to come back to bite you. You'll be asked about it under oath, and if you admit to it, every aspect of your testimony will be called into question. In an undercover case it's not the dealers who are on trial, since they're always guilty—you can't run surveillance on someone for eighteen months and accidentally get the wrong guy—it's the UCs. If our testimony or good character can be impeached, if we cheat or cut corners or colour outside the lines the dealer goes free. That's not even mentioning the attendant problems with focus, reaction time and sliding judgment that are the occupational hazards of the professional drug user. We're probably the only group of people for whom every drug is a gateway drug.

The dope business is almost exclusively a business of men, since so much of it is fronting—drug, money, attitude—which means that any woman you meet—at a bar, a drug house or a strip club—is going to belong to someone, because they all belong to someone. She might have had a fight with her boy-friend and decided to talk to you to make him jealous, in which case you've just slammed the door on that particular opportunity for investigation. There are lots of strippers or suitably messed-up women surrounding the drug trade, but if they're involved at all they're usually mules or lackeys. I've seen kingpins set up in a bar and have their strippers fulfil the dope deliveries—take the orders and come back around an hour later and drop off the merchandise—a precaution that failed to protect them in court. The women are usually just chattel—this is not an enlightened subculture—so anyone who visits this world knows that a woman will get you into trouble more quickly than almost anything else. I know of one UC who ended up banging a girl who was the sister of his number-one target, and the Crown would not proceed with the prosecution. Their attitude is, "We invest a lot of time and money putting you into play. You want to get drunk, meet some women, ring the bell? Go to another town—or fuck right off."

Of course, some undercover agents do go bad—dramatically, monumentally. Along the way I've heard whispers about dirty cops in Montreal and Toronto, all of whom later went down—dope, double-dipping, extortion, set-ups. A large part of the job is attitude (good or bad). We can all default to putting on the animal show if we have to, but some of these guys are just turned up to eleven all the time. That can't end well. Too much *Serpico* or *Prince of the City*. The first one I remember was The Doctor, who got caught smoking a joint in his dorm room at the Canadian Police College in Ottawa. Perhaps not the most despicable behaviour conceivable, but imagine risking a promising career on something that balls-out stupid. In civilian life he'd be the fellow at the craps table with the unhealthy pallor living for those six seconds when the dice are tumbling.

We had an operation fold when an undercover guy was buying dope from a main target, the target brought along his old lady, and she and the UC hooked up later. The whole thing ended there, except that she developed a conscience and told her husband, and he proceeded to administer a beatdown to the undercover. The target got off on all charges and sued the police, to boot.

Larry Houston was a financial guy in a large undercover operation who double-billed everyone. Made a plea deal and lost his job. Scotty Dogood (his real name) was a drug squad guy in charge of helicopter eradication efforts who passed the addresses of outdoor grow operations to an informant whose associates would take them down dressed as cops. Dogood got a piece of the take, and the victims were powerless to stop it. After the informant was arrested and convicted, Dogood visited him in prison. Although prison visits were rarely monitored, one of the guards recognized Dogood as a cop and, suspecting collusion, taped their conversation. So Dogood got a chance to get to know prison life from the inside.

Robo had a similar case: a dirty cop in a Toronto murder case turned out to be borrowing service revolvers and bulletproof vests from the police locker and lending them to a gang of Bulgarian ex-military who would knock over other drug dealers, then return the vests before anyone noticed they were missing. The Bulgarians recruited him out of his gym; they were all deep into steroids. The tell on how rare an incident that was is the number of cops who came out of the woodwork to get in on the takedown. Here's how Robo tells it:

> The takedown was the coolest thing ever. This was top priority for Toronto, who were pretty upset that their guy was involved, so we were doing surveillance, wiretaps, the whole deal. The day of the takedown these guys all went out car shopping in Niagara Falls—Mercedes-Benzes, BMWs, living the high life—when a call came in to them that there was a drug house they could take down. They lit out for the Danforth with us in covert pursuit, and it was like *The Gumball Rally*—we made the drive in roughly forty-five minutes, clocking in at two hundred kilometres per hour. They suited up in the bathroom of a McDonald's and emerged looking exactly like us. It was in an apartment complex nearby, and when they came out we swarmed them—there must have been fifty of us, all told. One firecracker or stray car back-fire and we would have had ten dead cops in the cross-fire. The only one who screamed and cried when they dragged him across the asphalt was the cop. He got eleven years in prison for that, and ten years later, when they all got out and picked up where they had left off, we did them all over again.

One of the more famous rogue cops in Canadian history was Jimmy Buckle, who was in the North Bay drug unit. He looked like Fabio, with long blond hair down to his waist. I met him early on at an internal hockey tournament that the drug unit guys held. He came up after me, and I saw a lot of myself in him. A lot of people did. He was just very convincing, very likeable, completely charming. It was widely believed that he would go far, that there were finally some guys coming up behind us who could take our place. Jimmy was the point man on a crew of crazies known as the Killer Bees who would show up at every undercover party in the province. These guys were definitely crossing the line—and then some. He and another guy bought their own police-regulation Harleys and began slowly customizing them on the company dime. He was billing $1500 a month for a safe house that rented for $800 a month and pocketing the difference.

Buckle was working an undercover project in Southern Ontario when he got sideways with dope and money. He was supposed to have about a kilo of cocaine in his evidence locker from a bust, along with his court exhibits, paperwork and everything else that he was required to keep on file. Except eventually, because of one thing or another, it wasn't. So he went in on a Saturday when no one was in the office and set the place on fire. I would wager that in his own mind Buckle was just a guy who worked hard, played hard and thought he deserved to have a hobby, but somewhere near the deep end he let go of the side of the pool. As Smitty says, "You gotta get used to working out ten feet of pole down twenty feet of line." People like Buckle are far outside the protection of police procedure, cover or backup; they're balanced over the shark tank, and when they fall, it's for good.

Smitty had a pretty spectacular flame-out himself. He got into trouble in 2003. He called it being sent to the penalty box. In another era the cop who stopped him might have used his discretion to take his keys, driven him home and not written it up. (Our immediate supervisors were like our den mothers or fathers, and when they sensed one of us spinning out of control, they'd say, "Oof, this isn't fucking good," and pull us aside to straighten us out.) With mounted cameras, GPS tracking and daily reports in use, the patrol officer is under scrutiny. That goes all the way down to speeding tickets. There are no secrets at that level. I'll always help a fellow cop out when the situation calls for it but not at the risk of my job.

In police work, once you're in the door, if you don't do something egregious or irreversible, you'll be there all the way up through a great retirement package, a golden pension and the guys singing "Danny Boy" at your retirement party. But fuck up badly enough and the first thing they do is ship you out of the drug unit the next day, and you find yourself in an ill-fitting uniform in some far-flung outpost. As is the case everywhere, your fate depends on what type of person you are, whom you know and if you're worth saving or not. The vast majority never make it back in because you find out pretty quickly who your friends are and who's prepared to let you flap in the wind. "We didn't like him even when we liked him." Oftentimes they'll just wait and see how you handle it. Do you cry like a baby, blame everyone else, disrespect your superiors and run everyone else through the mud, or do you take the bullet and do your time? (This is one instance where the criminal class can serve us by example.) Smitty did his time. Luckily he had a lot of equity banked. He came back to fight another day, which not many do.

From my experience I'd say the secret to understanding people who spend their lives combating drugs and drug enterprises, and who pride themselves on failing to succumb to the lure of drugs at close quarters, is that we live a life that's in itself extremely addictive. Traditional addictions pale by comparison. You can't say no to this job, and you can't get enough of it.

CHAPTER 5

SUB ROSA

Like any actor or anyone who lives in the moment, you learn that your best strategy is an insane amount of preparation disguised beneath a practiced cool. First rule of show business: never let them see you sweat.

Your goal as a UC is what we call peeling the onion. You need to get close enough to the primary target to strip away the layers of secrecy and subterfuge that he wraps himself in for protection—against outside threats like you, but also against the wolf pack surrounding him that would rip him to carrion at the first hint of weakness. Gaining his trust requires a degree of patience that comes only from experience. If you drop some stray fact into the conversation but contradict it eleven months later, a silent alarm goes off behind his eyes that you'll never hear. You've just given him a wedge to pry open your lies and your life, and your time will have been wasted. Whatever your target's secrets, it's safe to say he's practiced at holding on to them.

So you really have to make sure that your story is watertight—that it has a solid beginning, middle and end. Build a cover that doesn't raise red flags; it can't be so bland as to seem generic, but it also can't be so exotic that it invites attention. You're not a drifter or a salesman exactly, but you weren't a fighter pilot in the war either. Know your goals, what you're aiming for, how to exhaust one topic of interest in order to move on to another one that might prove more rewarding, as if you're sweeping and clearing a room. And always have an exit strategy—whether it's from a conversation, a room or a mission.

The easiest thing you can do to sell your identity is not to act like a cop. Remember, criminals watch TV just like everyone else. I like to start from the time I draw the assignment and first roll up on their world. In the early days, the preferred costume was jeans, a T-shirt and a leather jacket. No tattoos, dangly earrings, shaggy beard or biker regalia; too much thought has gone into that wardrobe already. You might as well show up on a panhead Harley with apehangers and a Captain America helmet. The more of the real me they see and accept, the less reaction time there is between me and my assumed identity. You never want to be too flamboyant since it makes you the centre of attention, but I've shown up for a drug buy in cutoffs, a Hawaiian shirt and flip-flops. When Smitty saw me he said, "Are you fucking kidding me? I can't take you anywhere." Except I was able to score more drugs than I ever had before because I was relaxed and more approachable. Meanwhile, Smitty was so intimidating in his full leathers and patches that people didn't want anything to do with him. With me, the worst that could happen was I might invite you to Disneyland. Piss Smitty off and he might leave with your head on a pike.

Pulling up to a bar you've targeted, you park right in front where it says No Parking. Just jam it in there without thinking twice about it. Why? Because no cop in his right mind would flout the law quite so casually. A Horseman would circle the block twice and then park in the municipal lot four blocks away. For him showtime begins when he walks through the door. Bad guys don't have showtime; they just don't give a fuck. Next, there will always be some troll mope just loitering about. Palm him a five-dollar note and tell him, "You see that car? If you see the ticket guy, come and find me." When Mopey comes and tells you, "The ticket guy is coming," you look like a guy who commands respect.

I had the luxury of growing up Irish, which means that long before I was old enough to shave, my uncle had schooled me in the etiquette of how to walk into a bar: "You don't look left and you don't look right. You look straight ahead, go right up to the bar and get yourself a drink. After you get your drink, you turn around and see who's there." The guy who walks into a bar with shifty eyes and a shuffling gait has just squandered his momentum.

In every bar there will be some poor lonely creature who will latch on to you in hopes of improving his social standing. If you give him the time of day he'll parade you around town and introduce you to all the players, just so he can bask in the momentary warmth of their curiosity. He'll also inadvertently sell you to these same players, claiming you're good friends, because you're his ticket inside their circle, even if it's just for a little while. That's how you always start out cold. When we roll up the project a year or two later, I always let these guys walk. It would be easy to snare them in the net like the pilot fish they are, but would justice be better served? These guys are collateral damage at best, whose greatest crime was that they wanted to be liked, so I refrain from buying drugs from them as a matter of principle.

It's generally harder to buy an eightball of coke in a bar than it is a half tonne of hashish coming in on some freighter. At the level where you're shipping it, each party will have been vetted to the other's satisfaction. When it's just the two of you, things get dicier: you've got a pocketful of money, hopefully he's got a pocketful of drugs and either one of you could be a narc. There's a gun or a knife somewhere, even if you don't need to brandish it. I've always been nervous going into a buy. Sometimes I know what I'm going to say but also where I'm going to take this guy—what my strategy is, and how much I'm going to get from him before I jump to the next level. That's what I tell the bosses anyway—sometimes I don't figure it out until I'm in the lion's den. You dispense with lower-level players as soon as you can: there are lots more of them, so they're effectively worth fewer points, plus you get more bang for the buck the further up the pyramid you get, since gravity is your secret ally, and they tend to take each other with them on their way down.

You can't buy too much in case the locals talk to one another. With coke, for instance, an ounce is a big buy—it would get your name mentioned around the bar. You try to keep everything a secret between you and the guy, but the further you get into the project, the friendlier you are with all the players—you're getting invited to the after-parties, hanging out in the daytime, you're one of the gang. Dealing drugs in these situations is extremely personal. If I buy an ounce one night from one guy and half an ounce the next night from another guy and they ask me about it, I'd better know why. If my cover story says I'm spending the next week up at my hunting camp I don't need an ounce and a half to do by myself. Buying from the same source over time can show that that first deal wasn't a fluke—it's one more way to blend in.

There's also a difference between doing drug deals up north and those in the south. Up north where the towns are smaller and more isolated you see the same people every night at the bar. There are fewer diversions, so more people are going to know your business. Walk into a bar for the first time and you're the new guy, so your job is to put everyone at ease and take the attention off you. Farther south toward the big cities the deals get easier and you're less reliant on your cover story. If you look the way they look, drive what they drive and can talk the talk, there's no reason for them to believe you're not one of them. Traditionally it's been money, dope and guns—mix any two of them and you've got a recipe for combustion. These days you always meet at least once before you do the deal, to allay first-date jitters, and you keep the dope at a second location where their henchmen can go and pick it up, all coordinated by phone. Having been through the meet-and-greet, I can often detect traces of fear during the deal itself. That tells me what I'm doing is working and gives me an opening I can exploit later. It's a bit of a chess game; ignore the larger patterns at your peril. And always know how many moves you are away from a showdown.

Another thing I do is always try to screw up the money. If someone targets you for a buy and you sense they're deep in the mix, tell them you don't have any cash. Narcs *always* have cash. Only narcs pay on time—not even legitimate businessmen pay on time—so don't be a chump. Make appointments and then fail to keep them, a tactic that annoyed my bosses to no end but seemed par for the course in the drug trade. When you can, seem fly-by-night and more than a little scattered. If I have to count out bills during a transaction I'll forget the count, drop piles of money in my lap, hand stacks of bills to the other guy while I try and remember where I was. I'd say, "Okay, let's see—two beers, a game of pool, you owe me five, so here's ninety." It's ridiculous but charming, and every time they roll their eyes is one less chance I'll take a tuning.

I also routinely insert what I call "intelligence-gathering nights" into my schedule; Smitty calls them "animal nights." Since it's a UC's job to buy drugs, and my job is to not get made as a UC, I would have nights when I refused to buy any drugs, regardless of what came up. I'd roll into the bar, get liquored up, not worry about taking notes on everything around me and let all my new friends see me with my hair down. At the end of the night I'd walk to the corner, and the cover team would pick me up and deposit me safely back at home. Most projects are stats-driven, so my refusal to buy is one more piece of evidence that I couldn't be a cop.

Over the duration of a long-term project your greatest asset outside of your cover team is probably your cover story. It explains your actions and, more important, your absences, and if it works right, it curtails suspicions about you before they arise. It's not uncommon to get a knock on the door at a safe house and one of your neighbours is there to welcome you to the block—the one who drew the short straw to put the bell on the cat: "How are you? It's kind of strange . . . all day long, this place is silent, but at night it lights up like a Christmas tree. . . . Mind if I ask you what you do for a living, anyhow?"

"Of course. We do night laser surveying. We can only work at night. By the way, when was the last time you had a survey done on your property?"

Redirect, redirect. Keep them off balance and unfocused. An hour later you're down at the block party eating barbecue, explaining the finer points of laser cartography.

Which is easier to do if you've worked something up ahead of time.

You always run the risk, no matter where you are, of being noticed when you'd rather not be. The smaller the town the more exposed you are. Smitty had a situation where two days before a takedown: he had a dozen guys ensconced in a safe house—twelve-gauge shotguns, battering rams—when the phone rang.

"This is Constable Dudley Do-Right from the city police," a measured voice said. "Would you please come to your front door?"

He peeked through the front window and saw there were a dozen police cars outside. He opened the front door and raised his hands, and when they leaned in to pat him down, he managed to whisper, "I'm a cop on assignment. Walk me in the back and I'll show you my badge." After they were satisfied the local cops saddled up and left, and Smitty had to call the deputy chief of the local police department, an old friend, to successfully keep a lid on things for another day and a half. Another time, up north in Hearst, we'd been out all night making buys and were up frying eggs when I saw some neighbours peering in the window. There was a scale out and drugs all over the table. Rather than try to explain, we just folded up the operation and were gone by noon.

For my part, the most nervous I ever got was when I had to pass through an airport in the company of a bunch of criminals that I was forced to travel with. Airports are designed to move large numbers of people through them quickly, and the chances of having your cover blown increase exponentially. The last words you hear could easily be "Bobby! You still with the OPP?"

Bars, restaurants and most public settings are at least manageable: position yourself with a clear line of egress, and you can usually anticipate any threat. Never go drinking at a bar where you bought drugs and took somebody down because that's just disrespectful—you deserve to get hurt. If you have a meet scheduled for a cop bar or somewhere they know you, call en route and say you've got a flat and have to reschedule. If you can, get to the meeting early and give it the once-over to defuse any surprises. Scotty was supposed to meet Ricky Diamond, a full-patch member of the Satan's Choice motorcycle club, to buy some fentanyl, a narcotic in transdermal patch form. While he was casing the bar before his scheduled rendezvous, the bartender recognized him from high school, saying, "Hey, you're with the OPP, right?"

Scotty went out and met Diamond in the parking lot. He told him, "There's a copper in there who's got it in for me. If he sees us together he's going to arrest us on principle."

I managed to avoid doing drugs during a meet or buy and it was a good thing, too, since it will always come out under oath. The easiest ploy is to feign some excuse: "I quit smoking; this will just get me started up again." "I can't be high—I've got an important phone call I've got to make / I'm seeing my old lady right after this / I've got a long drive home." If it's coke, say, "I'm taking that home to sprinkle on my girlfriend's tits." Or take the mercenary approach: "What are you, stupid? It's a fucking commodity, man. Only losers use that shit. I *sell* to losers." If you're smoking pot or hash, have a cigarette going and take a drag sometime before you have to hit the joint or pipe, then exhale the smoke. If you're outdoors it will be cold, so your breath will frost up. If you have to simulate snorting coke or meth, and you can get away, go into the bathroom, cup your hand under the faucet and snort the water out of your palm. Snorting water gives the same physical appearance as snorting powder—the same runny eyes, runny nose and sniffles.

Basically, in every case, you're trying to take appropriate steps to not be in a place where you shouldn't be—physically or rhetorically. It's like carving the elephant from a block of marble: you just take away everything that doesn't look like an elephant. Danger is your negative space.

And make sure if your cover does get blown you have a plan for what happens next. If somebody tells you, "I heard you were a cop," control the moment until you can see daylight. If you can't bark him down on your own, see if there are others present who can vouch for you or run interference. Keep talking; it's what you're good at. If your exposure window is seconds to minutes, you can try to use the referral shuck: "That guy who was just in here—I think he might have been a cop. There was something not right about him." If you have a callback to the same location, stretch it out to give yourself some cover: "Listen, that thing I said about that guy being a cop? I shouldn't have said that.

Forget I mentioned it." If a buy starts to go south, demand a do-over: "Man, I don't know you—you could be a cop. And you don't know me. Why don't we just dial it back: you give me back the money and I'll give you back your dope, and then neither one of us has to be looking over our shoulder. I don't need this hassle." They never take you up on it.

I'd walk away from a deal if it got too complicated, particularly the ones that never seem to end: "Let's meet at your house at noon," then "We'll meet the guy at the Pie House at two," which becomes the Keg at six, then the bar at ten. I'd tell them, "This is starting to smell like a set-up. You're just getting your ducks in a row to rip me off." Eventually you develop a Spidey sense—that tingling sensation that anticipates real danger, often by mere seconds. Part heightened awareness, part paranoia and part higher consciousness, it's the one thing that all UCs possess—if not starting out, at least with skin in the game. I never got the chance to talk to one of these guys after the bust went down, but I always wanted to: "What was going on there? Were you guys setting me up? Or was it a test to smoke me out, see if I would follow you around forever, which only a narc would put up with?" (Scotty got ripped once for five grand in Oshawa—some yahoos just disappeared with the money. His solution was especially elegant: he went to the best friend of his primary target, a Satan's Choice member who owned a tavern, and told him what happened. The tavern owner always had a soft spot for him—they looked alike—and intervened to get his money back. This got Scotty one degree removed from the target. Then he bought off the tavern keeper and jammed him up as well.)

In an extreme situation you can always opt for what we call the Full Smitty: he was in a bar on an animal night, and a guy he knew came over to him and said, "You want to hear something strange? My friend over there says you're a cop." Smitty went full–bore ballistic on the guy, roaring up to his table bug-eyed crazy, when the guy said, "Relax. You don't remember me, do you? You're that OPP narc with the long name. You and your friend in Sault Ste. Marie cost me five years." The guy's friends stood, waiting for Smitty to cold-cock him. Never one at a loss for words, Smitty executed the fail-safe move he had tirelessly perfected for just such a pre-dicament: he turned the table over and ran like water. The cover team parked outside saw him crash through the front door and had to catch up with him halfway up the block.

Often in an investigation, whether you're undercover or not, you'll have a confidential agent who, for reasons of his own, has agreed to co-operate. What seems like a straight-forward transaction on the outside is inevitably complicated by the state these people are in that's led them to this decision: their lives are in danger, they have money problems, drug problems, girlfriend problems—every problem under the sun. Most of them can barely balance a chequebook. Once you inherit them they become your responsibility. So I always make the effort to ask how's the wife, how are the kids, take them a Christmas turkey, a cellphone card or gas card, some tangible semblance of humanity, because everyone they know wants to rob, cheat or hurt them. I'm basically the nicest person in their world. We don't want to keep them like rabbits in a cage, living on a couple of carrots now and then, but as long as they put themselves in this cage we can at least try to make their lives a little easier.

The problem is that these people are rank opportunists with a chip on their shoulder and a dubious sense of entitlement. They will always take their best play, and if you're it, then hunker down because you're going over the falls. As much as a wink from one of us when he's making his deal is enough to overturn his case and put us on the hook for supporting him for life.

Consequently, the OPP has a separate division to deal exclusively with the agents. After the takedown and the project is retired, OPP handlers debrief the agent to see if the UC or his cover men made any promises or offered any special perks. Most of the agents I've talked to who've been through the process said it was far more stressful than anything they encountered working undercover. The whole premise behind it is to preclude the agent's lawyering up and chiselling out some angle to sue the OPP for false promises, and they are *very* aggressive in their questioning. At stake is potentially millions of dollars in settlement fees, and the thing the OPP hates most is spending money on adversaries who are cleverer than they are.

For my part I had to be careful not to say anything that an enthusiastic lawyer could twist to his client's advantage, while trying to be supportive and encouraging toward the agent on the outside. Remember, these people have basically just cashed out every friend they had, and you're often the one guy they have to turn to.

In my experience, one in ten makes it out of the life. The rest are either used to six figures a week and blow their 100k buyout before the first snow; can't stand the revved-down lifestyle and wind up dead or in jail; or fall victim to a vicious karma. It's a fine line for the UC to walk, and one more reason why we often confide in each other and no one else.

Generally a project is over with when the money runs out and you've gotten as many bodies as you think you can get. If your haul includes stolen cars, goods or guns, the natural inclination is to explore further, see if there are any robberies or murders hiding in the weeds. Those big-ticket investigations also carry a big bleed—all these things can spawn new police investigations, which can keep expanding forever, so a lot of time the bosses just decide to roll it up and call it a day.

In the time before cellphones and texting, when it was still possible to clamp down on information, we also used to do what we called a rip. This usually occurred at the end of the drug project, where we would set up a big drug buy, except instead of us turning the money over to our dealer, we'd arrest him instead. We keep our money, take your dope and you go to jail. Game over. Since the takedowns always occurred in the early morning hours, you would just pick your best guy and rip him the night before.

One of the biggest disappointments in this job, I would say on reflection, is that after eighteen months of extremely high-pressure work I couldn't be there at the takedown. It wasn't to protect my identity—I'd be seeing the accused when I testified in court, plus it'd be pretty clear who was missing as soon as everyone was in a holding cell together. But since I was busting people from as long as a year before or more, it was up to me to oversee the takedown packets—photos, known locations, MO, evidence to look for, threat-level assessment—and to be the liaison for the Tactical Response Unit in those situations where its use was called for.

All that clerical work has to be done clandestinely, or else you risk blowing the whole operation. All it takes is one patrolman who can't make it to a Friday night party because of a Saturday morning takedown, and he tells his wife, and she tells the hosts, and they tell the other guests – it can spiral out really quickly. It also makes for an extraordinary amount of tension, which is why most people who run these ops tend to rely on people they know they can trust. For the last month or so on any big operation, we work around the clock for the last month or so and turn the safe house into a de facto war room.

On the morning of the takedown there'd be a hundred lawmen jacked up and armed waiting in response teams at some ice rink or gymnasium at four in the morning, and the commanding officer would need to show me off as a prop to deliver a locker-room speech and launch them to their tasks. At this point I would have been up for forty-eight hours, running on pure adrenalin. The first doors would be kicked in around 6 a.m., and by 9:30 or 10 it'd be all over.

In the old days the UC would be waiting when they brought the targets into an interview room, in order to capture their response. But over time the thinking evolved that this was just rubbing salt in the wound, and that the potential for immediate or deferred violence was great. So we stopped doing it. This probably works better for everyone except the UC. It still means you lack closure.

The one exception is if you take the bust alongside everyone else, where it's engineered so that you wind up in a holding cell with some of your key targets, and you can get every last little piece of evidence. This is by far the most daunting assignment an undercover officer has to contend with. Incarceration of any kind is a pressure cooker of need and access, a kind of hyper-charged free-market capitalism where corruption is rampant and anything is available at a price. On the inside, the thing in highest demand is information. If even a whisper gets out that there's a UC inside, it's an instant death sentence—like putting a lamb overnight in the tiger's cage at the zoo for safekeeping. We all did jail jobs, as we called them, and we hated every second of them: no sleep, no appetite, eyes all over you, your threat detector on eleven, among a predatory population that is extraordinarily attuned to detect fear or weakness. Anything can go wrong, and if it does, there's no Plan B. It's harrowing.

Once it's all over, the UC has the takedown party to look forward to, usually held within the week, where you can high-five all the short-timers and compliment your takedown teams. Everybody's got a story to tell from the morning of the show, and they're all hilarious. Plus you finally get to come out of hiding—often to people you crossed paths with during your time working undercover. On one occasion, during Project Shaft, two cops in Marathon threw me out of the all-night truck stop where I was trying to get a hot meal, just because the waitress thought I looked like a problem. It was me, the waitress and the cook in the joint at three in the morning, and all I wanted in the world was a hot meal. I ordered my steak sandwich, she brought it to me and I was just getting ready to dig in when I saw that she had called the cops as a precaution, and now they were here to escort me off premises. I never even got to take a bite. And to add insult to assholery, at the door, the waitress demanded I pay for my meal. I was three-quarters of the way through the project, so I stayed in character and gave them shit in true shithead fashion, as only the righteously indignant can do. But if I ever needed a reminder why people hate cops, here was a shining example that I could take with me for the rest of my career, and I vowed from that moment on to always listen to the other side. A few weeks later, at the takedown, minutes away from go time, I spotted these clowns after I'd just given my big gung-ho speech, and they looked as if I'd just peed on their spit shines. Later they sought me out and were extremely apologetic.

Once you've done your last buy, the next time you see them will be in court, where their reactions run the gamut. I've had everything from people taking swings at me to mob guys laughing and saying, "Good on you, you got me." Most of them plead guilty because they know you've got them dead to rights. Some stay in touch with you and always express a grudging respect—it's the cartoon where the coyote and the sheepdog are best of friends until they punch the clock at the edge of the pasture.

Robo ran into a Satan's Choice guy he'd busted, in a corridor at the courthouse, and the guy pointed an imaginary pistol at him—"You'll get yours, pal." Everyone saw it, and they took him down right there in the hallway for threatening a peace officer. They just added the charges onto his sentence. Smitty had a guy in a psych facility who, when asked how he planned to establish self-respect when he got out, said he planned to get his old job back, spend more time with his girlfriend, get back together with his ex-wife and—oh yeah—kill Smitty. I've gotten word of a possible blowback twice in my career and been ordered to wear my gun at all times (which I had to go and find). I keep an alarm system on my house so as not to tempt fate, and I don't have mail delivered to my home. Beyond that I figure if they want to track me down it's not too hard. Most of these guys see it as a game, since most of them are gamblers to begin with. Holding a grudge against the casino doesn't make much sense to them either.

Mainly you want to let it go after you've given your testimony, because it's unhealthy not to. On your earliest projects your natural inclination is to stay involved: follow the trial, find out about the sentencing. You're invested in the material. That path just leads to heartbreak. There are so many things that can go wrong between arrest and incarceration, none of which you have any control over. It's a circus, and speaking from experience, I know it will drive you insane. The only thing to do is consider it a job well done, accept the praise of those few who know what you did and preserve it the way you would a rose in the pages of a Bible.

Your adventures are all in the future.

CHAPTER 6

THE NORTHERN TOUR

Coming out of Barrie and finally making my way to Thunder Bay I was on top of the world, headed where I wanted to be. Now that I would be working on my own I would develop the street knowledge and skill set that would see me through another twenty years down in the trenches and up on the front lines. I kept my teeth on everything so they were nice and sharp, and eventually I lit the world on fire. I affectionately referred to it as my Northern Tour.

Thunder Bay is a hard-core blue-collar city, a town that wants to punch you in the face. It's also the hub of everything: Great Lakes freighters, the Canadian National Railway, an international airport and the Trans-Canada Highway. If you're headed east to west in Canada, you're going through Thunder Bay.

The way the Flying Squad works is that you never live where you work. If you live in Thunder Bay you never work undercover in Thunder Bay, you're off in some far-flung safe house. Once you get out of the cities, Canada is primarily a resource-driven country: whatever can be scraped off the ice, dredged out of the lakes or dug out of the frozen earth, they're going to make a clearing and carve it into movable pieces, then ship it back to civilization to stoke the furnace for another winter. You get all these little single-purpose towns up north that are blasted out of the ice using the blow-torch of human tenacity, and rather than narrow it down I hit them all: Hearst, Kenora, Cochrane, Marathon, Kapus-kasing, Longlac, White River, Ignace, Wawa, Atikokan. But the first one was north of the Shield, and just about as cold as the place where Santa makes the toys.

Most of those fell under the umbrella of Project Sue, cen-tred in the pulp-and-paper-mill town of Dryden, which had the unnerving feature of always smelling like dirty diapers. In those days there were drug units all around the province—Kingston, London, Toronto, Windsor, Thunder Bay and one stray dog all the way up in Kenora, on the border of Ontario and Manitoba, and six hundred kilometres north of Thunder Bay. That one-man operation was Donny Birrell, a legendary lone wolf whom I had encountered when I was in Geraldton. Or rather, who'd seen me as free entertainment when he passed through a speed trap I was operating up on the highway, and I had my first high-speed chase. Donny had Allman Brothers hair and a ZZ Top beard, and he refused to stop. I chased him to a hotel, where he abandoned his vehicle and ran into one of the rooms. I followed him in, weapon unholstered, and there were all these Thunder Bay drug unit guys laughing their asses off while I tried to stop hyperventilating.

Since Donny worked solo he was always poaching Thunder Bay guys for the drug projects he worked up. He remembered me—I ended up doing drug intel for him while he was in Geraldton—so when I flew back from Thunder Bay he requested me for a really tasty project he'd worked up. I didn't even have time to unpack my bags. All I had was a room number at a hotel outside of Dryden, and when I walked in and, in my best Johnny Cash voice said, "My name is Sue! How do you do?" Birrell responded with a burst of manic laughter and said, "Thanks—I think I just found a name for our project."

One of my targets was a guy named Grant Finch, the self-proclaimed biggest dope dealer between Manitoba and Ontario and quite famous in the drug world. He owned a commercial hunting and fishing camp called the Polar Star Lodge on the shores of Lake Wabigoon. The camp consisted of a main lodge and half a dozen smaller cabins. He spent all his time up there with his family, where it was presumably harder for people to bring their sordid problems into his rarefied world. I rented a cabin in the off-season, and there was no one there but Grant, his family and me. I spent a lot of time with him, and ended up buying a tremendous amount of drugs from him throughout my stay. At the end of the project, we were going to rip him as the last score before the takedown.

In my time there I had heard him mention various caches of money and drugs buried on the property. If we did it right, at the end it would be an Easter egg hunt.

All the cabins were the same: a couch, a kitchen table, an old TV on top of the fridge, a bedroom on the side and a tiny bathroom. The very first time I ever wore a wire was when I stopped by his cabin to place my order for the deal where we would rip him off; it was about a week out from the actual takedown. Wearing a wire was just coming into vogue in police circles, and our electronics guys practically creamed themselves over the possibilities. They strapped this awkward thing to me—I wore it in the small of my back—with an antenna going up one side and the microphone going up the other. Not terribly sophisticated, and they never worked right.

In those days before cable TV you had your choice of CBC English and CBC French, often determined by which one your rabbit ears could pick up at any given time. For a noted dope dealer Grant was a teddy bear of a guy, probably aided by the fact that he was a notorious chain-smoking pot-head. When I got there just after breakfast he had the CBC English station on, and he was already buzzed. Definite Cheech and Chong vibe. As I said, "Good morning, Grant," I could hear my voice coming out of the television—the wire had reverse-engineered itself and begun transmitting over the nearest electronic device. I was halfway through my next sentence when it registered in my brain that I was speaking in stereo. Grant was so high that he had his own built-in time lag, and we both stopped at exactly the same moment. To make matters worse there was no kill switch on the wire, so there was no explanation I could offer without contradicting it over his TV. The moment just sort of hung there as we stared at each other. What should have happened was that he'd reach for a shotgun and cut me cleanly in half, then bury the separate halves with his money and his hash. But in Grant's world, high as a satellite, the odd sensory event was not altogether unexpected.

He said, "Wow, this stuff is really good," and I reached under my coat and ripped out every wire I could find, freaking out my cover guys hovering back at the treeline.

I've heard of guys who wore a battery-powered wire and it got so hot that it stuck to their back and burned through their skin, or the battery exploded and dripped battery acid down their butt crack. So I was lucky, I guess.

Grant was pretty amusing for a drug titan. He took me under his wing in the ways of the drug trade. He prided himself on always being able to spot a narc, and he used to lecture me on his technique. I was a rapt pupil and kept extensive notes, slowly spinning my persona away from whatever imaginary target he was describing. Those lessons probably saved my life several times over. He would have made a good adjunct professor at the Police Academy; he could have taught Crime 101. But first we had to get through the takedown.

Our electronics guys were extremely apologetic and quickly isolated the problem, assuring me that it wouldn't be repeated. A week later I was back for the rip, again wired so the cover team could hear me. Same deal as in Barrie: say "Florida"; get out of the way. On this particular rip, since we were out in the boondocks and everything in the vicinity was frozen solid, there wasn't any good place for the ninjas to set up. The fix our tech guys came up with was that they would lie down in the bed of my pickup truck and we'd throw a tarp over them, then they'd just wait for the go word. This was in the dead of winter in Northern Ontario, and these guys had driven like that from Dryden, a good twenty kilometres. Inside the lodge, it was just Grant and me, like we had been a hundred times before. I turned off the TV set—no Voice of God to complicate this round—and we got through it pretty quickly. Once he had handed over the drugs I told him, "Man, when this is done, I'm headed to Florida."

Nothing.

I said, "Wouldn't you like to be in Florida right about now?"

For the second time the wire was hanging me out to dry. I was reasonably panicked.

"I'd like to go to Florida, guys!" I shouted to no one in particular.

"You want to pay me or you want to talk about Florida?" Grant asked.

I told him I'd left my money in the truck and bolted out the door. When I dropped the tailgate on the pickup the ninja team exploded out the back like a ball of puppies and left me half-buried in the snow with boot tracks across my chest. The techs were apologetic once more.

The police dog showed up about twenty minutes after Grant was in custody and began scouring the property for his stash of hash oil. The dog found small caches of drugs and money, but nothing like the motherlode Grant always talked about having buried on premises. The dog was doing grid patterns from the fence line with its handler, but nothing popped. The handler kept saying, "I don't know, Bob. He doesn't seem to be turning up anything."

It was my first solo project, and everyone kept looking at me skeptically. I said, "It's around here someplace."

Then the handler fell flat on his face in the snow. There was a coffin-sized armament locker packed with small canisters of hash oil, and one corner of it had slipped up just above the ice, which the handler had tripped over. It was frozen solid, so the dog couldn't smell a thing. Yeah, nice work there, Scout.

We also took down a number of drug dealers who had regular day jobs and lives: the mayor's son at the mayor's house, the town librarian, a Grade 1 teacher. And Grant went to jail for a long time. When I saw him in court, he was as friendly as ever, as though we were still best buds. Or maybe he was still high and didn't quite realize what had occurred.

On Project Sue, through my friendship with Grant, which I made no secret of around Dryden, I got invited to the fabled All Tokers Curling Bonspiel—a seasonal blowout open to drug dealers and their families, like some Far North Freakers Ball. Once a year the drug aristocracy throughout the region pools its resources and rents the curling ice in

Dryden for a gigantic tournament where they can blow the roof off the place. If you don't naturally see the connection between winter sports and smoking dope, an All Tokers Curling Bonspiel is clearly the event to enlighten you.

My cover man on Project Sue, John Eden, is someone I'm still good friends with. My own private superhero on call, he looks like the picture on the recruitment poster and is as honest as the day is long. You couldn't find a nicer guy. I decided to take Johnny to the bonspiel as my guest. When I told him about it he became incredibly nervous; staring at my taillights for six months and living in the shadow of impulsive violence was apparently less of a challenge than being seen in public.

"Listen," I told him, "I'm their friend, and you're going with me. The only thing is, you've got to choose a fake identity. You can't go as you—they might recognize your name." The rule is, in selecting a false identity, so as not to become too fancy or ridiculous, you use your own first name and your mother's maiden name. In his case this came out as John Davidson.

The night of the big bonspiel, it looked like a circus inside—there were hundreds of people, many in eccentrically appointed tuxedos. It was like the annual porn awards in Las Vegas, with the same mixture of tradition and rebellion, and easily the best party of the year. At the end of the night they held a draw for a giant-sized bottle of rye. Everyone was scattered at banquet tables, half in the bag, when they announced the winning name: John Davidson.

No one answered.

I looked across the way, and Johnny was deep in conversation at another table with one of the targets. They read his name again, and still nothing. I was trying to catch his eye without drawing attention to myself when finally one of the guys at his table said, "John, it's you!" Man births cow; film at eleven.

Project Sue led directly into Project Shifter in Hearst, then Project Shaft in Marathon (which the suits renamed Project Prospect, Shaft being a little racy for the newspapers) and finally Project Hourglass, which was done in conjunction with the railway. They ran about a year apiece, and there probably wasn't a spare weekend between them; I just lit each new one from the smoldering butt end of the last. Up north, in addition to the regular staples of marijuana, hash and coke, I saw a lot of meth, as well as garbage sacks full of mushrooms, which are indigenous to British Columbia. In most of these small towns, we're obligated to respond if the detachment commander puts in a call to the OPP. Their whole town could fit on my block, so the locals can see the cops coming from far away. The OPP keeps a stack of these requests in their inbox, and as soon as a competent operator is freed up they start another one. Since I was digging my way out of the doghouse I couldn't get through them fast enough.

I named Project Shifter after the Hurst Shifters in the old hot rods, in honour of its host town (albeit spelled differently), naming rights being one of the privileges enjoyed by the point man on the ground. I started it in the winter of '87.

In Ontario everything from North Bay up is French, and Hearst was no exception—a French lumberjack/paper-mill town where they spoke English as a foreign language at best.

There were two bars: the rock 'n' roll dive bar in the Queens Hotel (every small town in Northern Canada has a central hotel called either the Queens or the Princess, usually a glorified rooming house), and a younger dance club that pulled in 90 percent of the traffic on weekends. I may be many things but French is not one of them, so a few months in they got me a French-speaking informant, a mover and shaker in his late twenties who was worth his weight in gold. Better yet, he got a job as a bartender at the dance club, and soon he was wired into command central. In Project Sue I had to put in agonizing hours studying the landscape, making patterns out of shapes and sensing where the lines of power coalesced. This time he could make a few gestures in sign language from behind the bar, and I had all I needed to know on everyone who walked through the door. It was like suddenly seeing the room in infrared, where the heat blooms just leaped off the screen. Soon the drugs began to flow. I once even did an entire dope deal in sign language.

My cover story in Shifter was that I was a gold prospector—I got to use all that lore I'd picked up from my time in Geraldton. I even got my prospector's licence. The French-speaking informant, my cover guy and I all lived in a tiny safe house; there was barely room to sleep standing up, so we always needed an excuse to disappear during the day, while we were ostensibly doing our "jobs." One nice fall day

I took these guys for a ride in the country. While we were wandering around killing time out in the middle of nowhere we broke open a couple of six-packs—and before long we had no idea where we were. Out of the blue we saw a truck headed toward us and flagged him over for directions. Turned out that he was our primary target, the dope dealer we'd been tasked with getting close to. Since I was feeling no pain I gave him a beer and we started shooting the breeze about prospecting, and soon we were like long-lost friends. Back at the dance club that night I bought drugs from him for the first time. I free-styled a story about how I had a mining crew I was buying for in another part of the province, just so he knew I wasn't trying to infringe on his clientele. No problem, he assured me. After that night, with the biggest drug dealer in the region vouching for me, people came to me. The takedown netted forty or fifty arrests.

Next up was Project Prospect, a.k.a. Shaft. Marathon, on Lake Superior just south of Thunder Bay, was experiencing a mini gold rush, so I kept the prospector story intact, but this time it was much more a *Deadwood* scenario. These were miners—not really big on etiquette. Everyone wore Harley T-shirts and leathers, but they couldn't have cared less about bikes, since it was negative freezing on the back of a motorcycle, and Harley season lasted about four days in July. The big thing was that if someone liked your shirt, you exchanged with him right there in the bar. It sounds stupid, but it worked out as a kind of rite of passage. That happened to me on day one.

Around that time my boss in Thunder Bay took over Kingston Drugs. When you get transferred in the OPP they send a big moving company, but there are certain things they won't put in the truck, like propane tanks and barbecues. My boss asked me to load up such "contraband" and bring it to him in Kingston. I would do anything to get back to Kingston, so I put his crap in the back of my truck and went to work in Marathon.

On my way back from Thunder Bay I passed by the turnoff to the Pic Bar on the outskirts of Marathon. The Pic had a massive rep as a drug den, and no undercover had ever made a buy there. I figured I'd rise to the occasion. Pic was short for some Indian name I'll never remember, and the hardest of the hard-core drug bars.

When I walked into the place it was like the Land That Time Forgot: drugs out on the table, whores under*neath* the table. Capitalism at its finest and most friction-free. I ordered a beer to give myself time to come up with a plan, but before I even got served, the guy at the bar next to me said, "What the fuck are you doing here?"

The first thing that came into my head was, "Well, I got some shit for sale in my truck, if anyone's interested." Half a tick later the whole bar was following me outside to see what I had to offer. What they didn't have in money I swapped for dope. By the time we were finished the truck was empty and I had about four grand in cash and contraband. Whatever I came up short in paying back my old boss, I knew I would make up on the story itself, which quickly entered law enforcement lore, and I've been dining out on it ever since. I called the new boss of Thunder Bay Drugs, the guy who was taking over, and told him I had just bought drugs out of the Pic Bar, and he was going to have to take the old boss shopping for backyard accessories. The story was all over the province by nightfall. I also took a lot of my payment in coke, which was our first inkling that there might be a whole other drug supply system in place in Northern Ontario that we hadn't anticipated. This realization led directly to Project Hourglass.

Project Hourglass was done in conjunction with the Canadian Pacific Police Service to target a cocaine-smuggling ring using the railway system, in what eventually turned out to be an inside job. I wasn't an investigator on that project—I was just a plug-in to cover the trains and monitor drops—but I stayed with it for six months or so. The project was so named because there was exactly one hour between stops all across Northern Ontario—from Schreiber or Nipigon to White River, say. The trip always took slightly longer by car, so we were constantly racing between stations: driving helter-skelter along the North Shore, and taking our lives in our hands with all the black ice and salt-crazed moose, just to try and photograph someone off-loading drug shipments.

Our point men from the CPPS were a Mutt and Jeff team that should have had their own sitcom: the quiet, slim Maxwell Smart–looking one had his paperwork in perfect order and knew the times and dates of every train; he was like a walking encyclopedia. His partner, a big Greek guy, wore nothing but Hawaiian shirts and flip-flops and looked like a cartoon explosion but was pound for pound one of the best investigators I've ever observed in the field. These guys were polar opposites, had been partners forever and fought like an old married couple.

Since the quantity we were seeing in the North was too much for a couple of guys to be selling handshake drugs out of the back of the caboose, this had to be a sophisticated operation involving every aspect of the railway system. The only way to determine how it worked was to wire up the common areas on the train—the engine compartment, wherever the employees ate lunch—and piece together how the scheme worked. The trains all had satellite phones on them, and we had those tapped as well, along with pay phones at every stop, which by law had to be observed whenever the wire was being monitored.

What we found was an inside job, a complete organization of CP crew members who were unloading the drugs in rail yards to other CP employees who would then meet the local drug dealers somewhere outside the station. We took the whole thing down just like any other takedown, except that rather than having to go and find them we just waited at the designated station and they came to us. We had them all on a wire so, working with CP officials, we knew exactly who to round up: engineers, brakemen, conductors. The company had to have backup engineers on hand to take over driving the train. Since CP was mainly concerned with shutting down smuggling on their trains and dealing with the employees who were involved, they had neither the funding nor the wherewithal to follow those drug connections out into the community.

It was about that time that the new head of Thunder Bay Drugs thought I had done too many undercover jobs in quick succession and that I needed a break, so he assigned me as a cover man on somebody else's operation.

I hate cover work. If you're on the team you want to start, you don't want to bat backup, or worse, coach third base. But I had no choice, so in deepest winter in downtown Thunder Bay I found myself sitting in a parking lot diagonally across an intersection from the bar where our Uncle Charlie had scheduled a meet. The car was running, since I was trying to stay warm. The local classic-rock station announced they would play *The Dark Side of the Moon* in its entirety, so I poured myself a rye and Coke on the sly and settled in. The evening was suddenly looking up. After a while I saw these two guys come out of the bar and start walking right toward me in a straight shot—right through the intersection. Parked next to me was a pickup truck with a Ski-Doo tied up in the back. As they got closer I saw they were smoking a joint, and when they got up to me—my exhaust was pumping, Pink Floyd wailing—I rolled down my window, and one of them said, "We're gonna take the Ski-Doo out for a rip." Fine by me. Knock yourself out. They drove the snowmobile out of the bed of this half-ton pickup truck, got it out on the street and then they were gone.

A little while later—we were getting toward the end of the album by now, probably coming out of "Any Colour You Like" and into "Brain Damage"—there was a knock on my window. I rolled the window down, and this guy said, "You been here all night?" The snow was obviously melted around my car.

I said, "Yeah, pretty much."

He said, "Did you see who took my fucking Ski-Doo?"

"Uh, no. I had my eyes closed, listening to Floyd. But listen, I gotta go, eh?" They took me off cover duty after that, before they had to charge me as an accessory.

While I was living in Kenora, about an hour west of Dryden, and working on Project Sue, I also met the woman who was to become my first wife. That first year in the North a uniformed patrolman I knew in Geraldton got married in Winnipeg, and I went to the wedding. My wife-to-be was one of the bridesmaids, and we hit it off. It was about a ninety-minute drive to Winnipeg, and on my days off we started to see each other. After a year we got married—a full-on cop wedding.

In retrospect I think it was all pretty rushed. Once I'd wrapped up Sue we moved to Thunder Bay; all the guys in the drug unit kept apartments in the same complex. This place quickly became our Garage Mahal for after-hours and down periods, and since I was married and had the biggest apartment, mine became our de facto clubhouse. The situation prevailed until about the fourth time we descended on our newlywed apartment—four drug operatives and their cover men—and she met us in the hallway.

"Those people can't come in here," she announced to a hall full of grizzled veterans. "I don't want them in my house again."

Everybody froze. This was not a crowd that was used to being told they couldn't come in somewhere, not to mention that they happened to be entrusted with keeping me alive the four-fifths of the time I wasn't there. I made some lame excuse, and we chose to forgo our debriefing session that week.

We lived in Thunder Bay for only a short while, and then my transfer to Kingston Drugs came through. But it all went downhill from there.

CHAPTER 7

FAT PAT AND CARMEN

I'd finally made it down south to Kingston Drugs. There are four levels of drug cases, Level One being the highest. These are the cases that target the major food groups and can take down an entire criminal organization. Most of them traditionally are run out of the south, since that's where most of the money and optimum targets reside (not to mention most of the population, commerce, transportation and so on). So up north—in Thunder Bay, for example—you can be on your own with a pickup truck, a log cabin and get by with a single cover man. Down south it tends to be limos, Beamers, Benzes, safe house and undercover house, surveillance teams and a lot more money at every stage, from buy-in to takedown.

The OPP Intelligence unit had reached out to the drug unit for a UC. They had been working an agent and had the intelligence ready—they just needed the right Uncle Charlie to walk into what was a turnkey operation. They had a hole that was exactly my shape, and Thunder Bay told them, "We've got the guy."

My previous boss in Thunder Bay—PJ, the guy whose stuff I sold out of my pickup—was now the head of Kingston Drugs, and he did a lot of the background work to facilitate my transfer. Smitty was also at Kingston Drugs by now, and a lot of people thought PJ was out of his mind for putting the two of us together again. We got a stern talking-to before we ever got started.

It was 1989, and I was twenty-seven years old. To my mind I was a year late, due to my detour to the North, so I was more than ready to make up for lost time. I had a wife and a home somewhere, but truth be told, I was edgy when I was at home. By this point being Uncle Charlie was easy; it was living the life of Bob Deasy that had become an effort. I only truly felt alive when my life was at risk, and staying alive meant always being fully aware of everything—assessing threat levels, spotting patterns and what was out of place in them, processing intelligence, and on and on in an endless loop—which proved impossible to turn off. Whenever I was away from my under-cover targets for more than a few days I wondered what they had learned in my absence, if I was falling behind, what they suspected, if they had found me out. It's like a kind of ever-present obsession that never completely goes away, except a thousand times more visceral. Taken out of that context I was a fish out of water, gasping for breath.

The OPP's Intelligence section, separate from the DES, had two officers, known as Jack and Grogger—not undercovers, just twenty-four-hour hard-charging plainclothes detectives—who had developed an agent inside the Italian mafia in Hamilton. (If an OPP informant performs a specific action by request he becomes an agent and undergoes a rigorous background check. Once he's been cleared for payment he goes into the data bank as a number and is referred to as such from there on out.) The agent, 38, had spent a great deal of time inside a federal penitentiary because of his life in the mob. A childhood contemporary of the people he ultimately took the fall for, he had been set up to deliver diamonds and furs from a major mob heist to a fence in Florida who was actually an undercover cop. His mob friends left him to twist in the wind in prison, where he had a lot of time to think. It would be difficult to overstate the animosity he felt toward them in the months leading up to his release. And once Jack and Grogger had spent a considerable amount of time in discussions with him, he told them, "I want to do the mob, and I'm willing to introduce an undercover."

On a typical year-long drug project you can bring down an entire distribution network, wrap up a hundred bad guys and feel pretty good about yourself. The mafia is into everything—the drug trade, prostitution, but also stock fraud, real estate fraud, extortion—anything, basically, that would make them money. Get on the inside of that and the possibilities fan out in every conceivable direction. Putting an undercover inside the mob in Canada had never been attempted before.

Our strategy was straightforward: 38 would bring me in at a low level, then every day Jack and Grogger would take him away and debrief him, while my guys separately debriefed me. Once our stories were in synch, Level One protocol was to get the agent out of there as quickly as possible, since agents can easily screw things up. Agents by nature want to help, they're already given to a certain exuberance, and before you know it they've volunteered all kinds of random nonsense about you that will trip you up long after they're gone: "You know, Bobby's got his pilot's licence." "He was a marksman in the corps." "He's a big Philadelphia Eagles fan." All these are death sentences if they sneak up on you.

I flew from Thunder Bay to Toronto, where I was picked up by two Southern Ontario drug enforcement officers whom I would come to know as Buff and Pokey. We headed east on the highway, and somewhere along the way we rendezvoused with a second car containing Jack, Grogger and 38. We all booked into a hotel in Ottawa, and my bosses told us to go off on our own and take as long as necessary to get to know one another.

For the next week, 38 and I carefully crafted a shared background and memories and got to know personal idiosyncrasies and private peeves and foibles—everything that would appear to others like a long-time friendship without coming out and saying it. We spent every waking moment together, trying to get our story tight enough that it merited an introduction to the mob. The stakes were obvious.

During one of these sessions we came up with the limousine angle: I would show up with a used limousine I'd picked up in some deal and parlay that into a job as their private chauffeur. The cover story of having a limo business met the core requirement that I wasn't tied down to any one place. Plus, what self-respecting mobster wouldn't want his own private stretch limousine on call?

The Golden Horseshoe cities of Hamilton, St. Catharines, Niagara Falls and Toronto are the home of Italian organized crime in Southern Ontario, so that was where I'd be based. This was also my first undercover assignment where I wasn't posing as a gold prospector or land surveyor or water-quality tester for the government. Here, I got to be a straight-up drug dealer and evildoer. My cover story was that I knew 38 from the drug trade in Ottawa. No business cards, no phone extensions, no professional credentials or references on call. It was refreshing.

In 1989, there were two family heads contending for the role of kingpin for southern Ontario, Pasquale "Fat Pat" Musitano in Hamilton, and Carmen Barillaro just down the road in Niagara Falls. Carmen was a chief lieutenant of John (Johnny Pops) Papalia, head of the Hamilton mob and a Calabrian affiliate of the Maggadinos in Buffalo, themselves a subset of the Bonanno family. Johnny Pops, born in Hamilton in 1921, was part of the first generation of Italian Canadians, born to Sicilian and Calabrian immi-

The main drag in
Geraldton, Ontario.

North of Geraldton
in Nakina.

The children's Christmas party in the detachment at Geraldton, c. 1984.
Dave Wall stands on the left and that's me near the man in red.

The Barrie safe house. Where it wasn't so safe in the basement.

At the Tornado takedown party. Back row is John Miller, Randy Carson and Bill Gigg, and that's me and Smitty in the front.

With Joey Montana

The Thunder Bay safe house, 1988. John Eden, me, Donny Birrell.

In Kenora, Project Sue, with John Eden and the TV that picked up my voice from the wire I was wearing.

Weighing dope and taking notes in the safe house in Hearst.

In front of the former Kingston Drug Unit with my Monte Carlo SS, a preferred UC ride.

Kingston Drug Unit, c. 1989. Smitty, me, Caper, Larry Willet, Millsy, Corky, Basil.

Kingston, c. 1992. Search warrant obtained, door kicked in.

OPP, RCMP and Kingston City Police in the Outlaws clubhouse after the takedown.

From my days with the Russians.

At a gathering of Para-Dice Riders in Port Perry.

GOOD FRIDAY '95

In the cockpit of Air Cannabis.

Yank, Mick, Scotty, me and Al Bush, along with my oldest son, 2005.

New York's finest giving directions to a bar to me and Scotty on St. Patrick's Day, 1999.

Jed, Cankles, Millsy, Smitty, Scotty and me in the Garage Mahal, 2011.

grants brought in during the manufacturing wave in Toronto after the turn of the century. The son of a bootlegger, Johnny Pops had been the high-profile godfather of Ontario since at least the 1950s, and was even a minor figure in the nascent French Connection heroin smuggling ring. With Johnny Pops diminished by age, Carmen was the de facto next in line of succession. Fat Pat's father, Dominic Musitano, a Sicilian, ran his own fiefdom with the blessing of Papalia and operated in his shadow for most of his career, until a heart attack side-lined him and allowed his sons Pasquale and Angelo (known as Ang) to come into their own.

Fat Pat and Carmen enjoyed a sort of détente, each oper-ating his own restaurant business: Carmen ran a place named Murphy's Seafood (go figure) in the shadow of the Falls, and Fat Pat was the proprietor of a bakery right in the heart of Hamilton. It was all very civilized. Except that whatever advantage they failed to gain in traditional turf wars tended to manifest itself as a petty rivalry over whatever the latest shiny object happened to be. And soon enough the shiny new object was me.

The way our project was orchestrated was that 38 would be returning to the fold after taking the bullet for these guys, and he was ready to work. This time he brought a friend along with him. With the Italians your actions always speak louder than words, so we showed up ready to play and open to suggestion. My attitude was that I wasn't going to talk my way into anything; I was an outsider—38's outside-in-the-car guy. I wasn't Sicilian, and these guys had seen every kind of hustler known to man. My job was to do what they told me and not ask questions—that's the front I put up to everybody I met. So I stayed outside with the other outside-in-the-car guys and bided my time. At this or that meeting 38 would tell Fat Pat, "Look, I've got Bobby in the car with me, and I just wanted to let you know we're here and it's good to see ya." Kisses and hugs, pat on the back and wait for him to bite. When we'd see Fat Pat, he'd always ask, "Does Carmen know you're here?" And whenever we saw Carmen, he'd ask, "Have you guys seen Fat Pat recently?" Without quite knowing it I was becoming the football in their rivalry, a way for them to keep score.

Once I was successfully embedded, another rivalry began to flourish. Behind the scenes, back in the land of bureaucracy, the head of Intelligence and the head of Drugs were locked in conflict as to what this breakthrough actually meant. Intelligence now had a transmitter in the corridors of power; they would be content to let it transmit forever. Meanwhile, Drugs wanted drug buys; they wanted to see numbers and bodies up on their wall. Since we were in blue sky nobody knew exactly how this would play out, so nobody had a sense of what to gamble for or how far to push it, and so these guys went at it twenty-four hours a day. I would get passive-aggressive messages from various subordinates down along the food chain: "We're shutting it down; there are no drugs yet." And then there would be a thousand phone calls and I'd get whisked back to Toronto for another high-level meeting. I wasn't in the mob yet, but I was in the parking lot, and that's closer than anyone had been before. Was my job to be or to do; to report or react; to be passive or become pro-active? Were we to play it safe or open the floodgates?

The problem was that these discussions were being made dispassionately, away from the glare of real-world consequences. Policemen can't resist the urge to put everything in a box, because once it's safely sorted and labelled, it makes sense to them and they can sleep at night. That way of seeing things was what drove me into a life of action rather than observation. This situation wasn't a controlled study, and it wasn't a metaphorical gridiron scrimmage. It was warfare, and your next move was always the one that kept you alive. Or not.

The same thing was true of jurisdictions, politics and who should come up with the money. All those concerns are paramount until the second you step outside into somebody else's crosshairs.

For instance, my first meeting at a table with these guys was between representatives of Italian organized crime, Haitian organized crime, two bikers and a Russian mobster. Run that through your spreadsheets and strategic directives and operational flowcharts.

After a few months of this tactic my innate courtesy began to pay off. I didn't speak unless spoken to. If we ate, I'd be the first one finished and have the door open and the car running for them. Whatever they were going to need an hour from now I would have anticipated and had it waiting. No funny comebacks, no stupid jokes—just protect and serve. And they ate that up like you wouldn't believe.

Fat Pat was obese and he was short, which made him look like a fleshy wrecking ball. He had fat, stubby sausage fingers and nails that were beautifully manicured. Always in an expensive suit, with lots of gold adorning his hands, wrists and neck, he'd say, "You see these hands? Not a day's work in my life."

The first time I met him in was at his bakery in Hamilton. It was small—a front room full of cassatini, small glazed pastries that looked like breasts, and cannoli, a word that for some reason always came out of my mouth as "guacamole." ("Cannoli, Bobby, for fuck's sake," Fat Pat would say.) Right off the front room was a smaller room where the associates congregated and awaited instructions, divided by a curtained doorway from the back room where all the high-level decisions were made. This was essentially the hub of crime in Ontario for as long as anyone could remember. Around the corner was a line of brick row houses, two or three of which Fat Pat kept as rental properties.

A couple of months in, 38 was talking with some of his associates when one of Fat Pat's guys leaned through the curtain and motioned me into the back room, where I'd never been invited before. When I made eye contact with 38, it confirmed that this was definitely not business as usual. As I approached his table Fat Pat looked up and studied me at his leisure.

"Bobby," he said.

"Yes, sir?" I answered.

"Bobby, I'd like you to take a walk with me," he finally said. He made no effort to alert 38, his friend of thirty-two years, and I followed him out the side door.

The bakery was located in downtown Hamilton, and I had a cover team and a spin team (tasked with surveillance) rolling footage right outside. As we casually made our way around the block toward his rental properties, I was ecstatic—not that I could show it—since I was finally on a first-name basis with the head of the mob, or at least he was with me. Simplest thing in the world: take a walk around the block—"Hey, Bobby, let me show you something." My first exclusive audience, and I was just about to step where no one had gone before me. Fat Pat carried a big ring of keys, which he used to unlock the front door of one of the row houses, and led me inside. My heart was pounding now, so I was concentrating very carefully on not showing any emotion.

"I'm glad I got you alone," Fat Pat said after he had locked the deadbolt. "I'm thinking of renovating this place. You don't talk much, but I know you're smart. I want you to help me. I value your opinion." He wanted me to help him redecorate. I had just become the official interior designer for the Italian mafia in Southern Ontario. As if I knew chenille from Shinola.

It meant I had gained Fat Pat's trust. He ended up losing interest in the apartment, but from then on I was Fat Pat's guy. He told me, "You don't need to bring [38] with you. How about you pick me up at nine o'clock in the morning?" I became his driver; he just wanted to have me around all the time.

In any high-stakes undercover operation I never had more than mere minutes to download to my cover what I had just learned. It really wasn't practical to wear a wire for that length of time, on the off chance that I'd be found out, so whenever they saw I was on the move, the cover car would fly by me and take me to some nearby quiet place, and I'd debrief my cover team as fast as I could. Then they'd rush me back to where they found me. It was like a Formula One pit stop; there were no movements wasted. If I needed a day or two away I would tell Fat Pat and the boys I had to attend to my drug business back in Ottawa and slip into Toronto for a face-to-face with my superiors, or check into a hotel suite so my intel guys could debrief me while Jack and Grogger debriefed 38.

Meanwhile, something similar was happening with Carmen in Niagara Falls. Carmen was a swarthy old-school mafia survivor in his late forties who maintained a private bar in the basement of his restaurant for visiting dignitaries. Upstairs at Murphy's, decked out in lobster crates, fish netting and various pieces of East Coast bric-a-brac, it was always crowded. But the massive downstairs bar sat empty, ready for an international mob confab. Sometime after I had graduated to Fat Pat's inner circle, 38 and I attended a major meeting with the Buffalo and New York families down the QEW at Carmen's bar. (For all their relative power, the Italians always claimed that they never had money, so dinner meetings were often at Carmen's restaurant.) Instead of keeping the drivers waiting in the parking lot, they had us stand just inside the bar this time. The other drivers were all Sicilian guys who were the same rank as me, most of whom talked among themselves in Italian. We were essentially like the waiters: one of the guys in the meeting would signal with his hand, a driver would run over and they'd whisper what they needed. I did that for 38, so he was on a par with the others. This marked the first time that someone in Canadian law enforcement had physically been in the room during a high-level meeting of organized crime, and the Intelligence guys couldn't have been happier.

Assessing what use I could be to him, Carmen made an offer to me and 38: he asked us to take the basement bar downstairs from Murphy's and make something of it. As Fat Pat had done, Carmen took a liking to me—my Intelligence guys were convinced he had a thing for me. The bar itself was over-the-top Italian ornate—dark wood, red leather banquettes, the whole nine yards. So we started brainstorming ways to get people into the bar: radio station promotional giveaways; happy-hour specials; tie-in events. We put in a DJ booth and a dance floor, new track lighting. We decided to use the black stretch limo to offer patrons free rides to and from the bar. I started driving the limo in my spare time, and when Fat Pat saw it, he said, "That's what I'm talking about, Bobby." From then on he had me drive him to meetings and started getting very demanding about my time, wanting me on call in Hamilton around the clock. Meanwhile, I had responsibilities with Carmen's nightclub an hour away, and this created frequent conflicts. I basically wore out the QEW going back and forth doing the bidding of both Fat Pat and Carmen.

After another one of the big meetings at Carmen's bar, as everyone else was queuing up the limos, Carmen approached 38 and me and said, "I want you two guys to go with Rocco here" (not his real name, but trust me, it suits him). Rocco stepped to the side entrance and beckoned us to follow him.

I knew there was a surveillance team outside, but since we were on the tourist strip practically right across from the Falls, it was a hard spot for them to get an eye, so they keyed on the parking-lot entrance to watch for my car. The bar had its own entrance just off the parking lot, and once we left the club we were immediately whisked into the back of a waiting Cadillac. The dozen limos in line served to cover our tracks; in the dark it would be impossible for anyone to see us leave. When my car was the only one left in the parking lot—the bar being closed for renovations in anticipation of our big reopening—the cover team knew they were in trouble.

As the Cadillac headed out of town, Rocco and the guy driving didn't say anything. We didn't know if 38 had taken a burn, if I'd taken a burn, if somebody put something together or voiced a suspicion and they were going to get it out of us with a baseball implement and power tools. We didn't know anything, so we couldn't do a thing about it. Ask too many questions, appear anxious in any way, and it's a tell—we might as well just confess. There was every chance it was a test, just to see what we would do, meaning that any effort to solve the problem merely confirms there is a problem in the first place. And we weren't far enough up the chain of command to demand any answers. Our only play was to wait.

Once outside the city limits we came to a hotel that was still under construction. The Cadillac turned in at the front entrance, where there presumably at least would be witnesses, but it quickly became apparent that the hotel wasn't open to the public yet. Instead of stopping in front we drove around back to a loading dock, amid scaffolding and construction cranes. I looked over at 38—a professional criminal who had weathered whatever prison could serve up—and I could see the fear in his eyes. This was not helping. I was terrified, but also more than a little pissed at all the mystery: This is how I'm going out? At least I had a right to some dramatic resolution.

The Cadillac stopped and Rocco got out and told us to follow him. We entered through a fire door that had been left unlocked and proceeded through the first-floor lobby, which was already finished. We followed Rocco down a corridor to a room with the door standing open. It was a double room, nicely appointed—I might have had some thoughts on the bedspread ruffles and the acrylic landscapes, but no matter. The beds were even turned down for us.

"Enjoy your stay," Rocco said, and closed the door.

Okay, now what? We looked at each other and, worried that the room could be wired, I mouthed the words, "Don't say anything." We went into the bathroom and turned on the bathtub faucet full blast so we could whisper to each other. I figured out a plan and turned off the tap.

Back in the room I asked 38, "Are you hungry? I'm starving. I'm going to go grab us some burgers."

Until then it hadn't occurred to me the door might not be locked. When I tried it, it was open. I walked to the lobby, and there was no one in sight—not even a security guard. The emergency exit opened. I walked out to the highway and still didn't see a living soul, then a couple of kilometres in pitch darkness until I finally saw the neon lights of what turned out to be a late-night Burger King. I called Al Bush, the head of my cover team, on the pay phone. Al was one of my best friends and the best man at my second wedding—and he almost broke down crying when he heard my voice. They had been waiting on point for my car to come around, and it had never showed. By the time they realized I wasn't coming out, I could have been anywhere—even dead. He told me later that it was the scariest night of his life.

When I got back to the hotel I had to tap on the window for 38 to let me in. I turned on the tap in the bathroom again and brought him up to speed. But now we also faced a dilemma. We could leave any time we wanted to. Except that if we left, we wouldn't be there when they came back to get us—or find out why we were there in the first place. Maybe it was a test: those who run usually have a guilty conscience. Whatever it was, again our only play was to wait. Obviously, we didn't sleep at all that night.

The next morning, bright and early, there was a knock on the door. When we answered it, there was Rocco, who told us our car was waiting. They drove us back to Murphy's;

again, nobody said anything the whole way. When we got back, Carmen was waiting for us.

"What did you think?" he asked us excitedly.

Frankly, we didn't know what to think. This seemed to confuse him.

"Yeah, but did you enjoy your night?"

Uh, yeah, sure.

"Great! That's my new hotel. I wanted you to be the first to stay in it." He appreciated all the hard work we'd been doing, and he wanted to do something nice for us. We thanked him and told him it was really sweet. But what we were thinking was, Could you not have fucking told us this last night?

In my heart of hearts I knew my first major crime was coming with Fat Pat rather than Carmen. Fat Pat was a year older than I am, while Carmen was considerably older, and there was a different kind of bond between us. Fat Pat would ask me, "So how are things in Ottawa?"—meaning, how's the drug trade.

I'd say, "They're good, but I could use a hand."

"I might be able to help ya," he'd answer. As casual as that statement seemed, for the respective heads of Intelligence and Drugs, what it represented was like scoring a touchdown in the Super Bowl. Although, as usual, each section thought it was their team that had crossed the goal line.

Fat Pat told me he was interested in some properties in Belleville, and he was considering converting one of them into a gaming house. So a road trip would be in order.

We planned to go from Hamilton to Belleville on a Sunday morning. After the viewings we would continue to 38's house near Trenton for a barbecue lunch. It was going to be a long day. My tech guys had already wired the limo, but when we ran a test nothing was transmitting, so I had to rewire the thing myself before I picked everyone up.

I had just driven east of Toronto when Pat announced that he'd like to visit some of the boys incarcerated in Warkworth. This was an unwelcome deviation in plans, one the surveillance team following me wouldn't be expecting. I turned the limo north from the 401, all the while thinking that the last place I wanted to be with a head of organized crime was the Warkworth Institution visiting room. The chance of my being recognized by inmates, guards or other visitors was too high. I told Pat that the trip was going to take hours and hours—Pat happened to be geographically challenged, which helped my cause. So Pat said fuck it and told me to turn around and stick with the original itinerary.

Meanwhile, in preparation for our arrival, a team was wiring 38's house for the meeting that afternoon. After we had finished viewing the properties in Belleville with 38, we headed to a coffee shop for a pre-lunch snack (he wasn't called Fat Pat for nothing). I excused myself and left them to prepare for lunch at 38's.

At the house the tech team was still busy with the wiring. I told them they had to get the hell out because Fat Pat was right behind us, but it still took them some time to finish up. They disappeared out the bathroom window at the back of the house just as Fat Pat and the boys were pulling into the driveway in a cab. I was running around in a state of panic trying to make sure there were no red flags in plain sight, when I noticed an electrician's tool belt sitting on the back of the toilet. I dropped it out the bathroom window just as everybody else was coming in the front door.

After a meeting with some mobsters from the States in the back room of his bakery, Fat Pat approached me about helping him smuggle weed into Canada in crushed cars. Among the Italians' many local business interests was a local scrapyard that had mountains of wrecked automobiles. Not that Fat Pat had ever been there. But it was an asset that fitted perfectly with Fat Pat's associates. Their plan was to load up decommissioned vehicles with dirt-cheap Mexican weed and crush them flat, load them into wooden crates and ship them to London, Ontario—coincidentally, the Mexican ditch-weed capital of the world.

"Can you handle it?" Fat Pat asked me.

What he meant was, could I take care of the quantity? Not, did I want a piece. If he got somebody to take it all off his hands in one go and could pocket his cut, that was the best-case scenario. If I was the guy to do that for him—he having observed me at close quarters on a more or less daily basis—it meant I was ready to move up. What he was asking me was, do you have the money? I told him as long as he always let me know the quantity so I could have cash on hand. Then we were off on a good old-fashioned drug negotiation, where

I was on solid footing. We settled on eighty grand for forty keys. In hindsight, considering that the weed was so bad, I was probably doing him a favour.

With mounting pressure from the Drug Enforcement Branch to start making bigger drug buys, we tasked 38 with broaching the subject of a cocaine deal: Fat Pat would supply a kilo of cocaine to get us started—at a considerably higher price than what I was used to paying. We would meet at a place called Prudhommes Landing on the waterfront along the Queen Elizabeth Way between Niagara Falls and Hamilton, right at the crook of Lake Ontario. There's an old pirate ship landmark washed up on shore. I was to leave my car in the parking lot with the money in the trunk and give Fat Pat a spare key. When I came back at 7 p.m., the money would be gone and the coke would be in its place. We did the deal, and then we were in play. The drug unit, naturally, was ecstatic.

The more I did for Fat Pat, the more responsibility he gave me. Now I was handling all kinds of things on my own, without 38 looking over my shoulder. This arrangement culminated in Fat Pat asking me to go for a ride, just him and me. There was a guy he had decided needed to be whacked—and he wanted me to do it for him. As we drove all over Hamilton, Fat Pat showed me where the guy lived, where he worked, his haunts and habits, all the while emphasizing what a piece of shit he was, and how the world would be a better place without him. I took this information in with perfect equanimity, as I do everything that's outwardly shocking: if you start to panic, they start to panic. But inwardly this confidence was as grievous as it was validating: at exactly the moment they trusted me to enter their inner ranks, it would all come crashing down because there was no way I could pull it off.

As soon as I could safely get away I reported all of this to Toronto. We gave some serious thought to buying the guy a new life somewhere else and pretending I had gone through with it. It was huge that I was far enough inside that they were actually trying to send me out on hits. But as with a lot of things, our best-laid plans wound up sideways once life got in the way.

It was decided that I would relocate to St. Catharines full-time, halfway between Hamilton and Niagara Falls. I would not be living in a safe house as in Barrie, since it was unlikely at this point that I could escape detection to return there on a regular basis. Instead, I would occupy a "UC house," which is a regular apartment that has been wired for full sound and/or video. I had to rent two units side by side, the second for a permanent surveillance team. The apartment manager couldn't seem to get a handle on it—"You want to rent two apartments? Side by side?" It was almost as difficult as setting up a drug deal—convincing people that you were who you were not.

I drove the limo as far as Belleville and stashed it, then went home to Kingston, while the Italians assumed I was shipping all my stuff from Ottawa. On the four-hour drive back, somewhere outside Toronto, I got a call (on one of the early Uniden cellphones) from one of my cover guys, who said, "Please go to Cherry Beach. Don't go anywhere else, don't call anyone, just drive straight there."

Cherry Beach is an abandoned factory waterfront right in the heart of Toronto where junkies go to shoot up, cheap hookers take their johns and bad cops take miscreants to tune them up. It's an ugly industrial harbour where ugly acts take place, and it's certainly nowhere you want to meet someone. When I got there my two cover guys were parked in their car looking really upset.

One of the men, Rod Carscallen (a.k.a. Buff), approached the car with a look on his face that could have meant everyone I knew was dead. All he said to me was, "Let's take a walk."

He told me 38 had been arrested for his part in an armed robbery of some safe-deposit boxes, and the project was over. "You're done," he told me. "It's already been shut down. Leave the keys to the limo on the seat, get in the back of my car and I'm driving you home to Kingston right now. He's gone bad, right off the rails, and we have no idea what he's said to anyone. We've got police guarding your house as we speak. We'll just have to wait and assess the fallout."

And just like that it was over, all gone in a puff of smoke. Everything I had done or been consumed by for the better part of a year no longer existed.

We drove to a bar in Kingston so I could try to unwind. There had been rumblings that 38 was unhappy—quite possibly due to the dithering over whether they were going to pull the plug. When an agent testifies and takes the cash, they relocate him wherever he's going, and then he never sees his family and friends again: mother, father, sisters, brothers, nieces and nephews all gone forever. He faced this moment on a weekly basis until he finally snapped. Who knows if he had made his mea culpas to Fat Pat and Carmen and asked for their forgiveness. In my heart of hearts I didn't think he'd burn me because he hated those guys for what they'd put him through. We had talked it to death before we ever started. But even if I was willing to stake my life on it, Toronto still wouldn't care what I thought. He had gone rogue; his word was worthless in a court of law, as was mine because he had vouched for me. He was uncontrollable, and the thing management hates most is what it can't control.

So I walked away. I went back to Kingston and was into a new assignment in a matter of days. In the meantime, a great many of my friends were in the middle of Project Retire, which involved the Outlaws motorcycle gang in Ontario. The project originated in Ottawa and culminated in the takedown of every chapter between there and London.

But there was to be an epilogue to my dealings with Fat Pat and Carmen.

Just over a year after I got pulled out of the mob I got a call from Toronto. Jack and Grogger had spent a considerable amount of time with 38 untangling the whole sordid affair and determined that throughout everything, my cover had never got blown. And now they wanted me to go back in. All I needed was a good excuse why I had disappeared for a year and never bothered to alert my friends, the Sicilian mafia, who were among the most dangerous organized crime figures in the hemisphere.

We reassembled the team, and then one day I just showed up back at the bakery. One of the ladies who ran the counter shouted through the curtains, "Bobby's here!"

Fat Pat's face parted the curtains with a kind of wondrous expression on it, as if he'd just seen a mythical creature. He didn't say hello; he didn't say anything. He didn't hug me or reach for a gun or react in any way. There was a phone on the wall with a rotary dial. Still watching me he picked up the receiver and dialled, then said simply, "Bobby's here," and hung up. Within minutes Cadillacs started pulling up outside, and the back room began filling up with people—all the boys from Toronto and Hamilton.

"Okay, come on in. Have a seat," he said noncommittally.

When the room was nearly full, Fat Pat finally addressed me directly: "So, Bobby . . . Where you been?"

"Out of respect for you, and you only, this is what I did," I began. "Are you familiar with the takedown of the Outlaws across the province?"

You'd have to live under a rock not to know what had been going on. Fat Pat nodded. "Well, all their dope was supplied by me. I know the entire gang, and my name has got to be out there somewhere. Nobody ever questioned me, but I know I was being watched. There was heat everywhere. If I had come back here—if I had tried to phone you or contact you in any way—I know I would have brought that heat to your doorstep. I couldn't do that to you. So although it grieved me greatly, I stayed away out of my loyalty to you."

Toronto had asked me a hundred times what I was going to say to them, and I hadn't been able to come up with anything. Or nothing I was willing to test run with the home office, anyway. It's a perfect example of what makes this life so intoxicating.

For their part Fat Pat and the boys thought this was the greatest fucking thing in the world.

I wish I could tell you that my acceptance back into their good graces led to the arrest of the entire membership of Fat Pat's and Carmen's crews and the decimation of the Sicilian mafia throughout Ontario for a generation; what Donnie Brasco did to the Bonanno family in New York City, Bob Deasy did to their affiliates the Papalias and Musitanos in the Golden Horseshoe. That would have been a pretty good ending. The drug guys and the intelligence guys were finally collaborating at full throttle; our team was psyched and large targets were coming into view. Jack and Grogger became my cover men, since there was no more 38. We all thought the planets were aligned for something historic to happen. And then . . .

And then . . . nothing. With the 38 prosecution pending, the Toronto brass was taking their cues from outside lawyers and became incredibly risk averse. The 38 situation continued to cloud any investigation going forward. After parachuting me back into the Hamilton cesspool, they decided—for a second time, and only one day after my re-entry—that the project was untenable. This go-round I pleaded with them to let me make a graceful exit, to leave an opening in case they ever reversed themselves again. It pushed the odds to talk myself back in the first time; it would be impossible to do it again. But the people who knew better than me overruled me, and I was informed that the project was terminated effective immediately.

After I said goodbye to my days in the mafia and went back to my life in Kingston Drugs, Fat Pat's father, Dominic Musitano, died of a heart attack in 1995, leaving the chain of command in Southern Ontario in question. Two years later Fat Pat and his brother Angelo masterminded a hit on Johnny Pops Papalia, by then a doddering old man, followed several months later by Carmen, which brought much unwanted attention to their activities in the region. Both brothers were eventually convicted of conspiracy to commit murder. Fat Pat was paroled in 2007 and currently lives a quiet life in Hamilton.

CHAPTER 8

PROJECT ENCORE

When the Italian project broke down the first time and I returned to Kingston, I was spinning in fifth gear all the time. After 38 fell off the edge of the world I needed something to take up my time and energy before my metabolism ratcheted up to a level that wasn't sustainable and the flywheel started coming apart. Smitty's standing joke for how we manage to cope with the stress is, "We drink a lot and drive fast." My boss PJ was the one directing traffic on Kingston drug assignments, and he threw me feet first into Project Encore.

Project Encore was a high-level drug operation with an agent attached to it, and it led me into contact with all sorts of colourful figures, including members of the Outlaws and the infamous West End Gang. This new assignment took place against the backdrop of Project Retire, which ended up taking down virtually every Outlaws chapter across the province—almost everybody I knew was involved in that to some extent. My part was more localized, but I managed to do some lasting damage.

Encore was launched when a well-connected dealer got jammed up on a small-time drug buy within our jurisdiction. Because his rap sheet was a mile long, even the most inconsequential slip-up meant he'd be going back to the big house for a good while. Looking for an exit strategy he cold-called the Kingston drug unit and asked them what he could do to help himself. He first had a meeting with Basil Gavin, who started by sussing out his motives, his contacts and what he could bring to the table. When Basil determined this guy had potential, he sent him on to two Witness Protection officers who conducted much more extensive interviews—and agent 391 was born. They reported back that he was the real deal: fully plugged in and ready to flip on his oldest friends, many of them high-level drug dealers in Ottawa, Montreal and Kingston. That was the landscape when I set out for a week-long assignment in Brockville, ready to rock 'n' roll.

I left Kingston in a dark grey Camaro Z28 on the way to my safe house in Brockville to meet Basil, my cover man. Basil's nickname was Father Time, and he was always looking out for us—a lovely man who was liked and respected by everyone he came into contact with. I was taking the scenic route along Highway 2 when I noticed a lone hitchhiker, a guy in his thirties, with his thumb out right at the entrance ramp. I was always glad for opportunities to alleviate the often soul-sucking boredom of the UC life, so I stopped and told the hitchhiker to get in.

The guy's name was Randy, and if you look up collateral damage in a criminal law textbook, you'll see his driver's licence photo. We weren't even to Gananoque when he steered us onto the subject of dope, and he volunteered that he was best friends with the biggest drug dealer in Pembroke, just up the road from Ottawa. Another one of those motor-mouth parasites that attach themselves to drug pipelines wherever they go above ground.

I said, "Well, I'm the biggest drug dealer in Pembroke, and I've never heard of your guy." This just wound him up even more. I was laying it on thick just to see what I could get away with, like rolling up on some guy in a bar to flex your bullshit muscle. But whatever grandiose claim I made, he wouldn't call my bluff. He thought he'd hooked the white whale. He wanted to sell me a pound of coke. By the time we reached Brockville I was over the novelty of hitchhikers, and I let him out at the first major intersection.

In Brockville, we had a safe house where we ran the project, and then an undercover house, which I pretended to share with 391, and where I first met him. He was a big guy but clean-shaven, more banker than biker, but clearly dangerous. I told him about my ride with Randy, and about his best friend, the Pablo Escobar of Pembroke, which 391 thought was hysterical.

Agents come in all flavours, just like the rest of the world. A few I've liked, most I've admired and some I've detested. But the one trait they all possess is that they're willing to betray others to save themselves. And since business—especially illegal business—is built on trust, and trust is best earned over time, that means they invariably betray the people they've known the longest, and possibly the best. I make it my business not to judge. But if they'd betray their closest friends they'd certainly betray me.

Agents usually become agents for one (or more) of three reasons. Vengeance: they want to get back at the people they're teeing up for you, and they relish every minute of it. Money: they're cashing out for good and need one final score. Desperation: they got caught with a hand in the cookie jar, and this looks like the least bad solution to their problem.

Even when they're being entertaining there's a certain perfunctory quality about them, as if they're giving you just enough to keep you interested and not a cent more. Since they can be extremely persuasive you have to constantly guard against coming around to seeing things their way, or else you'll find yourself too far down a bad road to get back.

The other reason you have to watch yourself is what constitutes the difference between an agent and a confidential informant, or CI. A CI is someone who gives you information. An agent is someone who acts on your behalf. It's a distinction that I've taught at the police academy, and it's often razor thin. If you give me a piece of information and

I thank you for it, you're my informant. You can never, ever be identified in court, and your identity is protected at all times, hence the confidential part. If you bring me information and I ask you, "Is it dark outside yet?" and you go and check, you're an agent. I can subpoena you and compel you to testify. But because you're beholden to me, it also means that now I own you. It is my responsibility to protect you from the consequences of these actions. And that can mean the difference between either a modest cash payment or life in the Witness Protection Program for the agent and his family, with us picking up the tab. At the end of the day they all want to trade up. Whatever they got paid, the money's long gone; if they've agreed on a settlement they want a better one. The difference is often largely semantic.

Agent 391 possessed a combo of all the motives to be in the agent business. He was going to take full advantage of the Witness Protection Program, and he was looking for payback against his crew for the way they had treated him. He was also one of my favourite agents ever because he kept his part of the bargain and didn't treat the deal opportunistically in any way. He was also the agent who was about to take me to some of the highest-level Eastern Ontario drug dealers.

We needed a way to get into the Outlaws' clubhouse in Perth to meet with Billy Scarf, just up the road from Brockville. I'd been waiting for this moment for a long time. Earlier that afternoon I had 391 stop in to see Scarf without me. I'd given him my cellphone and then I called it from a pay phone at a bar in Perth at an agreed-on time, screaming about a coke deal that had fallen through. Scarf took the bait and told the agent to go and get me.

The moment we walked into that isolated house at the end of an insanely long cul-de-sac—one road in, one road out—we were on our own. Our cover man, Basil, was trapped more than a kilometre away. When that biker coldly asked Scarf whether he was sure about me, time stood still. Feeling frozen there at the centre table, waiting for Scarf to weigh the odds against us, was easily one of the most harrowing moments of my career.

Sometimes if you let yourself get in situations like this it comes down to a straight bet: flip of the coin, even odds, fifty-fifty chance, no tears. This time it came up heads. Scarf was in a good mood, and not even the drug-fuelled paranoids around him could rattle him. Skeeter came back in with the coke we'd settled on, and I paid my money directly to Scarf, meaning he was done.

I bought dope from Scarf a couple of times during my year with Encore, as icing on the cake, and he bragged about all kinds of unspeakable things the police suspected him of but couldn't prove—murders, attempted murders, bank robberies, you name it. When they finally put him away he stayed away; he didn't even go to trial. None of them did, the big ones— they knew they were toast. And Lyle McCharles, the O.P.P. detective inspector who had it in for Scarf, sent me the biggest bottle of rye I'd ever seen.

———

Not long after we had become inseparable, 391 and I were sitting around the undercover house when the phone rang. He took the call and held out the phone to me.

"It's the hitchhiker," he said.

Like any good salesman working the leads, Randy was calling to see if I was interested in that pound of coke. He could have said they had a special going on, for all I remember. I told him to call me in a week. And he did— every week, along with the rug shampoo guys and the tele-marketers. I had dealers calling me up practically giving it away. The guy was relentless—he would not stop calling. So, fine—we set up a buy. I asked Randy what his friend's name was, and he said, "If I tell you, you're just going to cut me out of the deal." Randy was not making it easy on himself. I gave him my solemn promise that he would be part of whatever went down. If I had to I'd pay him out of my own money. We agreed on a price of $22,700 and set a time and place—a motel on the 401 on the outskirts of Brockville. We were supposed to meet at six at night. I was there with 391, and Randy was supposed to show up with his dealer. Six o'clock, knock on the door, Randy—but no dealer or drugs to deal.

"Yeah, little problem with that," said Randy. "He had to go into Ottawa. But he's on his way back. It's cool. You got the money?"

I was just about to lay into him when 391 picked him up and pitched him into the hallway. Our cover team guys were next door, and we could hear them snickering through the wall. If he would get the message and go wait in the car, Randy might live to fight another day. But no, two hours later he was back at the door, this time with the dealer but no drugs. The dealer explained to us, "Oh, I just wanted to see if you guys were for real." By law, if you represent drugs as ready for sale or transport, whether you traffic them or not, you're assessed the same penalty under the legal principle of "held out to be." (They are held out to be for sale, so the law recognizes them as such.) It's rarely used, since drugs are plentiful and it's just as easy to take them off the streets. But technically we had them either way.

I said, "I should have known you guys couldn't put together two Aspirin in a pharmacy. You're wasting our time." We made to leave, but the dealer turned apologetic and said he was waiting for their arrival; he asked us to let him go back to Ottawa and he could be back within the hour. So with our spin team in pursuit, they hightailed it to Ottawa to the home of a known coke dealer whom we had already bought from. Another two hours and these guys were back again. The cover team next door had already alerted us that we couldn't flip these guys for their suppliers since we'd already got them wrapped up, so this deal was essentially worthless to us strategically, and it had taken only eight hours to complete. We were stretched out on the bed watching Shark Week.

I took the money and slammed it on the table. The dealer started to count it, but he clearly had no idea what he was doing. It was like watching your four-year-old try to make pancakes. But it was a crime, we witnessed it, this was our job, we'd go through with it.

Then it came time for the trial. Most dealers, if you've got them dead to rights, just plead guilty and cut their losses. But these two clowns dug their heels in at every turn. I begged their attorney to plead out because I was embarrassed to testify against them in open court; they'd be blackballed from the Drug Dealers' Guild. I think Randy got three years and the dealer got six, and on the way out of court, Randy whispered to me, "Bob, I'll still do a deal with you after I get out." He still didn't get it.

Agent 391 would lead me into all sorts of crevices and cul-de-sacs. The guy immediately above him was named Billy Cole. A truly despicable human being. He cheated 391, cheated his underlings, tried to cheat me when I did deals with him—a self-styled Al Capone who gave the criminal element a bad name. He couldn't say two words without adding his personal endearment, "Cocksucker Face." Everyone he ever met, with the possible exception of his own mother, he called Cocksucker Face. He would do home invasions and rip off his own employees. The next day when they showed up and said they'd been robbed, Billy would tell them, "I don't care if you got ripped; you owe me $40,000." He forced 391 to go with him on these night raids. They would bust in with hoods over their faces, pistol-whip the guy, tie up his girlfriend and then Billy would say, "Okay, gimme the dope, Cocksucker Face!" The guy would say, "Billy, is that you?"

Billy had all kinds of ways to maximize his profits. Any time he got hash he would cut it in half, mix it with rabbit shit and press it into bricks with whatever was at hand; 391 actually did this with him by jacking up a rusty old school bus. Another of his schemes was to go to the library and steal a hardcover book that weighed roughly a kilogram, glue the covers to the pages, then cover it all with enough hash and rabbit shit to make a realistic-looking brick. He'd turn around and sell it for $7,000 a kilo.

Billy also took raw spaghetti and cut it up with toenail clippers and sold it as "purple LSD hits." He would dip it in grape Kool-Aid, bag it up and then do a Greyhound bus hand-off, where the buyer gets handed the drugs through an open bus window. By the time he realizes he's been taken, the Greyhound is hours away. And when I took Billy Cole down not a soul was sorry to see him go.

You never know what's behind the next door. When agent 391 walked me into a house in the outskirts of Brockville I met yet another high-level drug dealer. The guy lived with his mother, who must have had him when she was in her teens. I was doing a dope deal at their house one evening, seated at the kitchen table and weighing the coke on a set of scales, when the guy's mother, who was morbidly obese, sauntered out of a bedroom in a flimsy negligee. She looked like a wrapped ham in the deli section of Sobeys, and she would flirt with anything that moved. She sat down at the table just as I was about to make the buy, and her son, who was already pretty high, said, "You want to do a bet?"

I said, "What's the bet?"

The guy said, "If you can guess how much one of my mom's tits weighs, the dope is free."

I told him, "I'll take that bet."

Whoever came closest without going over was the winner. If I lost I'd have to pay double. I guessed four pounds, and the other guy guessed fifty. His mom was more than game, and plopped one enormous breast down on the scale. It topped out at twenty-five pounds—half a Labrador retriever. The number was small enough to win the bet for me but still large enough to give me nightmares.

I had another deal during Project Encore. The guy I was buying from thought that if he gave a kilo brick of hash to his kid in diapers and had him trot it over to me, it would protect him under the law. Turns out, not so much.

As time progressed it got to the point where I would see other drug dealers in my day-to-day life and we would nod at each other, a sign of grudging respect. The further up the chain you go, that world gets smaller and smaller, and I was being recognized as one of a finite group of regional players.

Through 391 I met a guy named Dave Snowden, who owned a picturesque tavern called the Duke of Wellington pub in the small town of Prescott, just between Cornwall and Brockville. The place was tiny, but Dave himself was gigantic—six foot eight and easily six hundred pounds. When 391 first approached Dave about our buying a pound of coke, Dave advised him that his price for making the introductions was a car.

Dave was partners with a guy named Roy Kirkey, a major figure in Montreal's infamous West End Gang, an Irish-Catholic crime organization that originated in the ports of Montreal—mercenaries and stone-cold killers who took Communion every Sunday. Roy's coke came right off the ships from Colombia with the original Spanish-language wrapping still on it, and it was so pure you could cut it two to one. The first time I saw him he was sitting at the bar at the Duke of Wellington sipping a brown cow. Roy was six four and 550 pounds—he and Dave could have worn the same suits—and 391 told him we could set the world on fire if we could just find a new connection who wouldn't screw us around. Roy said he understood. After huddling with Dave he emerged with an offer of $36,000 for one kilo—a sizable deal for people who didn't know each other. He told me to call him.

I did call him two days later—and the next day, and the day after that and so on for a week. He was always apologetic, and he always seemed to be on his way back from Montreal, but it took us through the Christmas holidays to get things set up and back in the same room together. It turned out that Roy was like the Santa Claus of the St. Lawrence, delivering his snowy treats to every little town between Montreal and Kingston. When we finally saw him a week later, he had just done five towns and still had three to go. I deposited a plastic bag containing $36,000 in a freezer in the pub's kitchen and followed Roy and a guy named John to the Burger King on the 401, where a runner had parked a gold

Ford Probe. John returned from the Probe with two packages of five hundred grams each. They were rock hard and wrapped in masking tape and resembled quarter-inch pieces of plywood, which is how they came off the boat from Colombia. I put them under my front seat and we drove off in different directions.

Rather than buy Dave the used car he had named as his price, I put $2,000 in a Christmas card and gave it to him at the bar. He always liked me after that, and counselled me to be careful about calling Roy, since the RCMP could build drug cases just by analyzing your phone bill. Henceforth, when I needed to order keys of coke, I would call the pub and reserve a table for one, table for two, etc., depending on the quantity.

After a couple of deals went smoothly, Roy tried to bring me in on all kinds of deals involving stolen merchandise: he had stolen Cadillacs and Mercedes-Benzes he brought up from Fort Myers, Florida; synthetic cocaine he called "the orphan" whipped up by his private chemist. Or he'd call and say, "Bob, do you want a load of Moen faucets?" Uh, thanks, no. "How about some crystal?" (He didn't mean speed but cut-crystal tumblers, one of which Roy kept in his bathroom, since he had it coming out of his ears.) After a while I felt that I needed to say yes just to avoid him getting suspicious, so I agreed to take a tractor-trailer's worth of stolen Levi's jeans—somewhere between fifteen and twenty thousand pairs.

Headquarters, of course, was less than enthusiastic about advancing us money to buy stolen Levi's that would come out of their drug budget. I wanted to keep the supply chain going with Roy at all costs, so I came up with a wild idea: I called up Levi Strauss and Company in the U.S. and asked for their head of security (and those guys are always ex-cops), and was transferred to Knoxville, Tennessee, where Levi's has a factory. I identified myself and asked him if he was missing a tractor-trailer full of jeans.

"Quite a few, actually," he said.

I told him, "Well, I've got at least a couple of them."

I gave him Roy's asking price, and he said, "Give me your bank account number." Turns out it was a bargain for them to buy back their own stolen merchandise at black market prices. We were heroes to Levi's, and they invited me down to tour the plant as their guest. At one point, on one of those long weekends of undercover work, two friends and I got a wild hair and drove all night to Knoxville to take them up on it. We essentially showed up on this guy's door-step, and he got us a suite at the Hilton, where they treated us like princes. Took us out for steaks with a bunch of his ex-cop buddies. Whole thing was stellar.

At the bar one night Roy asked me why we were moving so slowly. He had an unlimited supply of product at $30,000 a kilo, and I was his ideal customer. If his man in Brockville could move a kilo a week, I should be able to do at least that much in Toronto. I told him everybody works for somebody, and my boss, a guy named Gordy, was very careful with his business moves, and I was frustrated too. Roy told me he knew Gordy from eight or nine years ago in Toronto, back when he ran a cable company. He asked me to get him on the phone. Thinking fast, I called Jack, one of the two intelligence agents who worked 38 with me for the Italian mafia, at home in Toronto, praying he'd catch on. I greeted him as Gordy and told him I was here with an old friend of his from his TV days in Toronto. He got on the phone and they talked for about ten minutes, and Roy came away totally convinced that my Gordy was his long-lost friend. Everything was easier after that.

Of all the agents I ever worked with, 391 is the only one I can remember who got away clean. He was our property right up to the time we turned him over to the RCMP to enter Witness Protection, and he hated those guys so much he refused to go with them. We drove him to Toronto's Pearson International Airport and checked into a hotel suite for a 6 a.m. flight. I got up at 4 a.m. to get him ready, and he was in the wind—his bed wasn't even slept in. Two years later I got a letter with a picture of him in it. He'd written on the back, "Everything's just fine." He'd relocated himself.

As 391 eased out of the arrangement, leaving me to handle things on my own, both Dave and Roy would ask after him periodically. I told them he was dating a stripper, and that Gordy disapproved because he viewed strippers as a business liability. We had distanced ourselves from 391, and I advised them to do the same. Later on I told them he was facing charges on an old drug bust, and that he was lying extremely low. Dave volunteered a surefire way out of his predicament, which he called a "patch"—slang for patching a deal with the cops: the cops are always looking for publicity; they can't help themselves. We buy a gun or some dynamite and bury it in a schoolyard. Then we report it anonymously to the police. We offer to give them the exact location in exchange for their dropping all charges against our man 391. Once they make a big production of finding the contraband and protecting innocent schoolchildren, they'll suddenly be instant media heroes, and no cop can resist that. I told him I would pass it up the chain to Gordy. Later Dave followed up and told me he could get me a machine gun for between $4,000 and $5,000, but I never pursued it.

In the spring of 1990, for cyclical reasons, coke grew gradually scarcer and the price began to ease upward. I told Roy that Gordy should have $100,000 by mid-March, and he informed me that my price was now $50,000 a kilo, so Gordy's hundred buys us two. Despite previous assurances from Dave, Roy refused to front us any product, since now it was a sellers' market and there was none to spare. With a virtual cap in place on the amount of product we could realistically get at any one time, and with the coke coming from Montreal, where the OPP surely wouldn't spring for a joint drug project with the Sûreté du Québec, we were at an impasse on how much further we could get up the supply chain. So with the take-down imminent, we decided to do a rip on Roy and Dave.

I set up a coke deal worth a quarter of a million dollars— at that time the most expensive drug deal in OPP history. With minimal grumbling Toronto approved our flash roll of

$250,000 in cash. While I attended to last-minute details, the takedown army—spin teams, ninjas—all gathered in Kingston. Toronto even requisitioned the OPP helicopter. "We're worried about ya," said one of the top brass who had mysteriously gathered in Kingston to cheer us on and presumably be on hand for photographs. Of course I'd been there for a year on my own, while the $250,000 had only been there forty-eight hours. And after that first photo op I never saw the chopper again. Still, it was a nice gesture.

Dave had been curt with me in our last few phone calls. In person he said that the Horse was up on our phones and there were red flags everywhere. I was not to call Roy directly until this thing was over. The way the deal was structured, I would go to Dave's pub and show him the money, then he would call Roy in Montreal, who would drive down for the deal. I put the money in a black briefcase and placed it in the trunk of a fellow UC's car, and we drove separately to a Canadian Tire lot near the Duke of Wellington pub. I then went and got Dave and brought him over to survey the money—twenty-five stacks of $10,000 each. Since it would take Roy a couple of hours to make the drive, we went back to the safe house to wait.

When I returned, Dave told me Roy was very upset that I'd brought somebody else along for the deal. I said Roy must think I'm brain-dead to drive around alone in the countryside with a quarter-million dollars in my trunk. It wasn't all my money, and these people would take it personally if I compromised their investment. Dave suggested doing the deal in stages to keep everyone calm, while my man sat this one out. I told him I'd do it however he wanted, although it would take all night.

But Roy was spooked, and now he wanted me to come to Montreal and do the deal there. After I'd left the pub, as a last-ditch effort, I called Roy and asked him to meet me at a Texaco station on the Quebec-Ontario border, where we still had jurisdiction. He freaked out that I was calling him and told me to stop talking. Come to where he'd given me directions, he'd find me, bring as much money as I wanted and don't say anything else over the phone.

"Yeah, okay," I said, "but my friends might pull their money, so I can only commit to two [keys]."

"Fine—stop talking!"

Since the Sûreté and the Montreal police were standing by to take down Roy at our proposed rendezvous, I phoned Dave to inform him that we could still do the deal for the other three kilos here. We'd do it just the way we originally planned: I would bring him the money and give my guy the keys to a car parked at the Burger King. (The cocaine was actually sewn into the back of the seats.) My guy would go pick up the coke, call me with the okay and I would give the money to Dave. (This was so the money and the dope were never in the same place at the same time; if anyone got popped, it would be with one or the other.) In the middle of the deal "my guy" (actually a cop) called me back and said there was no coke in the car. Dave told me you had to cut open the upholstery behind the front seats.

The cop said to me, "Okay, we've got it. Don't give him the money."

Right. I've got that part. I hung up and smiled. Now all I had to do was wait for the ninjas to explode through the door—and in minutes there were masked men with guns in every doorway and it was all over. Dave flashed me the oddest look I've ever received—fury, awe, remorse, resignation and bemusement, like playing cards riffled in front of me so fast that I could only separate them by their afterimages. If I could show you that expression, it would tell you the story far better than I could.

Montreal was more than happy to give Kirkey back to us, since his crimes were mostly within our jurisdiction, so Basil went up to get him. On the ride back to Brockville, Roy rode in the back seat, all 550 pounds of him, and oncoming traffic kept flashing their lights at Basil because they thought he was driving with his high beams on.

After the takedown of Project Encore I worked on a few other projects, the most prominent of which was the Lynda Shaw homicide. Lynda Shaw was a university student who was driving alone from Toronto back to school in London in April 1990 when she was murdered. Her last-known stop had been a convenience store on the 401, and then her car was found on the side of the road just outside Woodstock with a flat tire. A search was mounted, and her charred body was found five days later just south of the 401 in a cornfield. She had been raped, tortured and murdered. By that time my marriage was on its last legs, and it was much easier to stay at my apartment in London and put the extra hours into a murder investigation than go home. This marked my first homicide investigation, foreshadowing the later post-drugs half of my career.

The OPP still had ten or twelve persons of interest, most of them involved in the drug trade, and my part was to make buys from them so the OPP could trade immunity for information on the homicide. They were kind of a loosely aligned gang, and the idea was to flush out any stray talk that was out there. There was no tie to drugs on Lynda Shaw's part, but that corridor of the 401 was a major trafficking route, and these people were in the business of keeping tabs on their surroundings. The case was one of the most famous in OPP history and by then had generated thousands of leads, none of which had panned out. At this point they were willing to try anything, even hypnotizing motorists to see if they could remember a second car. Female undercover officers posted ads on ride boards. There were endless lists of people with criminal records, people with violent histories, people whose stories didn't line up. But nothing was shaking out.

I thought the whole thing was screwy. If a person was involved, or had information that could make them an accessory after the fact, no one is going to flip on a drug beef to implicate themselves in a homicide. There was just an air of desperation about the case after a while. I made a dozen cold calls: for one, I had to find a way to get in with a guy who worked at a flower shop in a London mall, so my front was a high-end airport taxi service. I arranged with him a daily purchase of fresh-cut flowers for my supposed fleet of cars. Eventually I found a way to steer the conversation to the subject of pot. Another of the persons of interest had an auto repair service, so I knocked out a taillight and showed up with a pallet of "stolen" cigarettes in my trunk. This ploy led to other types of crime, which got us to a drug deal. Twelve successful drug buys, without making any of them suspicious. But nobody knew anything about Lynda Shaw.

It wasn't until 2005, fifteen years after the murder, a cold case team turned up a DNA hit for someone named Alan Craig MacDonald who, amazingly, had been paroled in 1989, a dozen years after murdering a cop and another witness. When he was arrested in 1994 with stolen property after a high-speed chase, and then released on parole, he took a shotgun into a phone booth and blew his head off.

While I was undercover in Kingston I wrote the promotional exam and passed, which meant I attained the rank of corporal. When that position was phased out I became a sergeant. At the end of my tenure in Kingston Drugs, a job opened up in Toronto as officer in charge of the CFSEU—Combined Forces Special Enforcement Unit. I put in my application and was accepted. Before I left Kingston, Smitty and I, on one of our many late-night drives on the 401, tried to figure out how much money we could get our hands on if we punched the Eject button. It was long past business hours and we had the keys to the kingdom—the evidence lockers where they parked the drugs, the safe where they signed out the buy money, our charge cards, bank accounts, untapped identities. The master fund. Six figures easily. Seven? Certainly enough to disappear forever.

CHAPTER 9

THE KING OF MOROCCO

The Combined Forces Special Enforcement Unit is an amalgamated unit of the finest law enforcement resources that can be brought to bear within Southern Ontario and the Greater Toronto Area: the OPP, the RCMP, the Toronto police and those from the three regional municipalities of York, Durham and Peel. Since I was bumped to sergeant after writing the promotional exam, the rule was that I was no longer eligible for undercover work. I'd had a good run, and this was the pathway to the next stage of my career. So I prepared to transition to criminal investigations—to work nine to five as a detective rather than months undercover as a feral beast.

But first, practically the day after the Italian project cratered, Smitty got a call from an old friend in the Montreal police named John White. He was working a joint project with the RCMP and the Sûreté du Québec provincial police centred on the Port of Montreal, and he was looking for a UC who could handle a one-on-one meeting that was already set with a major hash smuggler. Smitty comes from Montreal, speaks fluent French and has tons of contacts there. They had a big fish on the hook, and they just needed the right guy to walk into the party. Smitty told them, "I'm sitting here looking at him." He drove me up to Montreal himself in the middle of the night. We didn't file a project plan; we didn't tell anybody.

We all routinely volunteered for each other's assignments when they came in over the transom. It kept things in the family, and it kept your skill set sharp. It's just that we usually stayed within our own jurisdiction. Minor fucking detail, as Smitty would say.

They referred to the target as the King of Morocco—he was small in stature, of olive complexion, always immaculately dressed and spoke with an indeterminate accent. I don't actually know where he was from, but the King of Morocco seemed to fit him—royal carriage, intensely polite and with access to a medieval variety of torture, should he need it. He wanted to smuggle major shipments of hash into Canada from Pakistan, and he thought the Port of Montreal was too hot. He was looking for someone with connections who could move it through Customs at the Toronto airport. We were to meet him at Mont Gabriel, a ski resort north of Montreal in the Laurentians.

When I got there the place was completely empty. They had rented out the entire ski lodge for the day so we could meet in privacy. An agent, whom I never met, had represented me to them as an importer-exporter of contraband. It was snowing when John White dropped me off at the base of the mountain, and I sincerely hoped they would not find my body there come the spring thaw. They were waiting for me at the lodge—the king and two henchmen who stood in wing formation behind him with their wrists crossed in front of them, two hulking button men a size too big for their expensive suits. It was like a job interview. The king's name was Gabé and he was so soft-spoken that I had trouble hearing him. The alpha dog of his two goons was a Québécois named Greg, and he picked up the slack in attitude by constantly gunning me—picking apart everything I said. Gabé would ask, "What would you do about this? What would you do in this situation? Do you think you could handle that?" And every answer I gave, Greg would then challenge me on.

I told them my father worked inside at Customs. At the end of the meeting they took my phone number and said they would be in touch. I thought the meeting had gone well, so the first thing I did when I got out of there was call this lovely old guy I'd known at Canada Customs since I was a baby narc, Clay Titterson. He had a remarkable talent for getting almost anything through their bureaucracy without putting you waist-deep in paperwork—a skill he shared only with law enforcement, by the way. Working with him I set up an entire operational import-export business, with all the moving parts in place, the details of which I was prepared to share with Gabé when he called. Then I waited.

And waited. I never heard back, and when I took the job in Toronto, it became just one more of my elaborate might-have-been career bests. *C'est la vie.* (That's French for fuck all y'all motherfuckers.) Luckily, there was enough to do at my new job that I didn't have time to think about it.

The CFSEU does only high-level organized crime projects targeting the major food groups. I would be working on Italian organized crime, since I had just spent a year and a half undercover with them in two separate instalments. This was a very small, select unit—six-man teams with members representing each of the participating organizations; members brought their resources to the table and you followed wherever something led you—soup to nuts. I remember one project involving a coke-smuggling ring with freezer trucks that left Toronto with frozen fish, made the whole loop through the Florida Keys and then returned with frozen fish packed with cocaine. CFSEU had contacts in Scotland Yard, the DEA, Interpol—you name it. And since this was like the United Nations of crime fighting, we always put our best foot forward, so there was always plenty of money. We could put up wires, follow whoever we wanted—all those resource-intensive things that make accountants go green around the gills. And of course, having been promoted and made my peace with leaving the life of an Uncle Charlie behind, I was no sooner ensconced in my new mid-level management position than they assigned me my first undercover. It wouldn't be my last.

There was an organized gang of Somalis who were running most of the parking lots in downtown Toronto. They were stealing credit card numbers and pressing new counterfeit credit cards, then charging as much merchandise as they could before the victim realized what had happened and cancelled the account. With no actual card being lost or stolen, it was often a week or more before the theft was discovered, allowing the gang to spend to the card's limit. Since the object was to spend as much money as quickly as possible, the purchases were generally big-ticket items—electronics, major appliances—which they would then fence. CFSEU arranged a job interview for me at Eaton's, at that time the flagship department store in the Eaton Centre mall in Toronto. I showed up at their HR department and kind of skated through the interview, only to realize that they hadn't been alerted that I was a cop, and I was expected to land the job on my own.

Once employed, I was expected to infiltrate the gang through the parking attendant at Bay and Dundas and let him know I was receptive to their scam. The only problem was that I had thirty seconds with him each day before my shift to make small talk and convey my position. Meanwhile, I became insanely busy as an electronics salesman; the stuff was flying off the shelves. Since I was working primarily on commission, and I'm competitive, I quickly started to become one of the characters in *Glengarry Glen Ross*. My second month there I made salesman of the month.

And soon after I had let it be known to him where I was working, he showed up in my department with a stack of credit cards and I ran them through our machine to see if they were good. With the ones that passed muster he purchased stereos and plasma TVs, leaving me a couple of stereos in the trunk of my car as payment. When that crew went down I realized I worked harder selling subwoofers and big-screen TVs than I did ensnaring the bad guys.

One thing we did at CFSEU was build elaborate crime databases—a sophisticated version of the kind of busywork I'd spent my spare time on in small-town Geraldton. If you're investigating a crime, you shouldn't have to start from zero every time out; knowing the lay of the land and who the players are can save the next guy weeks or months—even years—down the line. So a lot of the work we did didn't end in dramatic takedowns or photo ops. It also took us to the unlikeliest places.

Case in point was a joint task surveillance detail I did with the RCMP on Eddie Melo and Harold Arviv, following them all over Toronto. Eddie (Hurricane) Melo was at one time a genuine contender, a middleweight and later light heavyweight Portuguese boxer who grew up in Toronto and won his first fourteen professional fights, twelve of them by knockout. Convicted eight times on charges including extortion and weapons violations, he moonlighted as an enforcer for Vic Cotroni, head of the Calabrian Cotroni family who controlled Montreal and most of southern Quebec through the 1970s, after having forged an alliance with New York's Bonanno family in the 1950s. By the mid-'90s the Cotronis shared power with the Sicilian Rizzuto family in Quebec, and Melo served as a kind of flag-bearer for the mob. Harold Arviv was a slippery character with ties to Israeli organized crime who once bombed his own A-list Toronto disco, Arviv's—for which he received a three-year suspended sentence—and had been implicated in penny-stock manipulation, counterfeit gem sales and a whole host of exotic schemes.

These guys were inseparable and into all kinds of stuff together, and we had a spin team up on them forever, which I was working on. We were coming up on Easter, and as the long weekend approached, more and more of the guys begged off to spend the holiday weekend with their families, until finally it was just me holding the fort. At the end of one typical day following these guys all over town, they took a cab to Pearson airport and got out curbside. I abandoned my car and followed them inside, where they proceeded through U.S. Customs and boarded a plane bound for Las Vegas. I called my boss, Larry Tronstad, a Horseman known as Tromper, and told him these guys were on the move, and he said that whatever I did, make sure I got on that plane. While I was in the air, Tromper called his old friend Bob Conboy in the Las Vegas PD, who was used to fielding calls from law enforcement liaisons all over the world, since Vegas is like Disneyland to criminals—everybody ends up there eventually. By the time our wheels touched down they had a full surveillance team standing by, and I joined the circus for the next ten days.

These guys went everywhere and met with everyone. I stayed in a six-thousand-square-foot suite at the MGM Grand where they had filmed scenes in *Rain Man*, while our targets parked themselves down the Strip at Treasure Island. They seemed to know everybody—a who's who of international crime, with key players from Israel, Germany and European ports of call, all duly photographed and documented by me and the Las Vegas surveillance team. That information then fed the Catroni investigation and a hundred more that I never heard about. As for Melo, he would survive a number of assassination attempts but ended up dying in an apparent mob hit outside a social club in the Toronto suburb of Mississauga in 2001. After an earlier falling-out over a stock deal, Arviv failed to show for the funeral, claiming that he was travelling outside the country at the time.

From CFSEU, I was transferred to Toronto Drugs. Toronto was the biggest drug unit in the OPP—not staffwise, but certainly in the amounts of drugs and money that flowed through there—and I had a wide network of Uncle Charlie contacts in the GTA.

At the time my wife worked at a medical company in the city and essentially had her own life, and I stayed on the job as much as I could, always volunteering for late shifts and weekend detail. To be fair, I had probably been home six months total in six years of marriage, and in my absence she had gotten her MBA at Queen's University in Kingston, in addition to raising our two kids, so it wasn't as if she was sitting home knitting. Maybe it was inevitable that we would have spun apart eventually. While it had always been easy enough to ignore our issues, now the wheels started coming off the cart, and a permanent rupture was imminent.

The OPP and the Toronto police had a long-standing relationship with the storied Amigo Squad, which was definitely the big leagues of drug work, since it focused 100 percent on Colombian cartels. The Amigo Squad was our designated liaison between Toronto and the OPP, and I was the OPP portion of it. What I hadn't anticipated was that the Greater Toronto Area unit differed from the OPP in one key way: they didn't have a fraction of the money that we did. What Toronto did have was expertise: knowledge of wiretaps and extensive information and background on Colombian cartels. They needed our help as much as we needed theirs.

Toronto has an immigrant population even larger than that of Miami (regarded as number one on a list of American cities with foreign-born residents), including a considerable number of Colombians and Jamaicans. More important, the U.S. "war on drugs" had done such a good job jamming up their own borders that Toronto became the logical entry point for Central and South American drugs. With nine out of ten commercial shipments to the U.S. from Colombia being flagged simply because of their point of origin, it was actually more cost-efficient for the Colombian cartels to use

Toronto as a transshipment point and bring the drugs into the U.S. across its northern border. So a number of Colombian businesses in Toronto became fronts for the coke trade. We found a massive clearing house for VHS tapes where they could fit a kilo of coke into a single videotape cartridge. I did a number of major projects with the Amigo Squad at their invitation. These were largely wiretap operations, except that everything was in Spanish, so we had to use designated listeners. The wire room would be filled with Spanish-speaking women translating wiretap tapes through headphones. Also inside the room were always two or three Spanish-speaking cops, who we called the "inside dolts," since they rarely saw the light of day. It was their job to listen to the most cryptic parts and try to decode the special mix of Spanish, English, Colombian slang and coded in-crowd idiom that by definition excluded us, then bring the latest revelations to our attention. Once, one of them was stumped and asked me to listen to a particular part, saying, "I cannot for the life of me figure out who they are or what they're talking about."

When I put on the headphones I recognized the speaker's voice as a guy I had recently come across in Toronto Drugs who ran a Persian rug business. They were substituting the names of rugs for quantities of cocaine. Once it was decoded, we discovered that tired of delegating these tasks to others and coming up short on product, he was going down to Miami himself to retrieve five kilos of coke from a storage locker. Not only would he be a sitting duck, but arresting him in Miami would remove the suspicion that we were running a wire. I phoned the liaison officer there and notified him, as a courtesy, that I would be in the Miami area on official business. I couldn't carry a weapon, and I had no official jurisdiction, but anyone in the crime business for any amount of time would have contacts in Miami. I knew people through the HIDTA group, which stands for High-Intensity Drug Trafficking Areas and comprises DEA, Secret Service, Border Patrol and U.S. Coast Guard agents, and they met me at the airport. With a group like that you get one-stop shopping, and once I'd laid out what we knew and they had cross-referenced it with their intelligence, they did what needed to be done to remove the impediments and hit it like a blue tsunami—a full SWAT team, people falling out of helicopters. Miami got the collar and looked like heroes. I went back down for the trial in the hope that he'd help himself and give somebody else up, but he pled guilty and took the pain.

Since the Amigo Squad was wiretap-driven we were constantly stirring the pot or poking the bear. The wire would give us the location of a drop, where a car would be parked with coke in the trunk, and we would go and steal the dope, then seal the trunk up as if nothing had happened. Then we would sit back and listen to the fireworks on the wire: a mid-level transporter had just lost ten or fifteen kilos of someone else's drugs. He'd have a meltdown, call everyone who worked with him to explain what just happened, then call anyone who owed him a favour who could airlift him out of the hole he was in. Now we had all of them on tape as well. With a ghost loose in the machine, he'd want to make sure everything was locked down—the stash houses, fake condos, rental storage units where he stowed the drugs and incriminating evidence—and we would dutifully follow him on his rounds. Then we would break in and liberate the dope there as well, increasing his problems tenfold. Everyone blamed everyone else, and no one suspected the police could have been behind any of it.

Our strategy took the drugs off the street, which was our prime directive, but it also sowed doubt among all the parties, which was a wedge we could constantly exploit. An operation like the Colombians' is run completely top down; every decision is made at the executive level, and all parts of the network are in constant contact through the chain of command. It would have been impossible to place a UC anywhere in that pipeline because he would have needed to be Colombian, and they would just have vetted his story at the source and then murdered his extended family. You had to wait for someone inside to flip. Our job was to speed up the process.

The Amigo supervisors would meet every morning at six or six-thirty to formulate a plan for the day and go ahead and do it. If something hot and heavy came in on the wiretaps we'd drop everything and put out the fire—and that happened almost daily. We shared money, people, resources, vehicles, information and strategy. It was a well-oiled machine, and probably the best unit I ever worked in.

Generally a court-ordered wiretap goes up for sixty days. You can get an extension from a judge as long as you have continuous evidence—when you can show that a deal is well in progress. The investigations led in so many different directions that by the time the court order was up, there was enough intelligence for a whole new wire and cast of targets. And each time we got to a takedown, the Colombians' legendary severity worked against them: faced with thirty years in prison—or worse, extradition to their native Colombia— the rats would line up to jump ship. This was twenty years ago, and that project is still running. It was the most beautifully run operation I've ever been a part of, and it has been an abiding principle of my law enforcement strategy ever since: the greatest enemy of the police is bureaucracy. Share everything and you share victory. We didn't stop the flow of drugs into Canada, but I think we stopped the Colombian cartels from gaining a foothold in the country the way earlier immigrant groups did in less vigilant times.

Pearson International Airport, Canada's largest airport, serves Toronto and the Golden Horseshoe, home to approximately 9 million people, and four times that number pass through it in the course of a year. Unlike New York, Miami, Los Angeles, Montreal, Vancouver, Houston and many other large international cities in North America, it is landlocked (Lake Ontario notwithstanding). The only real large-scale way for product to enter Toronto is through Pearson. So in addition to our participation in the Amigos, we set up a full-time Joint Force Operation to focus exclusively on Pearson. Joint force members included a lot of the usual suspects: Toronto police, Peel, the RCMP, OPP and Customs. The unit focused on intelligence gathering and enforcement. One such investigation generated enough evidence to launch a wiretap on baggage handlers. We uncovered an elaborate network of baggage handlers who were orchestrating the transfer of constant substantial quantities of cocaine and marijuana from Jamaica to Toronto every day. Through the wiretap it came to our attention that we should look at a particular Air Canada jumbo jet—a 747, which seats over four hundred—that was scheduled to arrive over one Easter weekend from Kingston. At the last second we prohibited the baggage handlers from emptying the transport hold and boarded the plane with a team of agents as soon as the passengers had debarked. Airport security had provided us with special purple all-access passes, and we merely pulled up curbside, swept through Security, past the various airline checkpoints and personnel and onto the loading ramp into the plane. The flight attendants and pilots were just gathering their belongings and tried to stop us from executing a search warrant, claiming they were technically still in international airspace. I said that was fine if they wanted to think that, but as far as the law was concerned, anything we found on the plane belonged to them. They didn't stick around to continue the discussion.

While our team searched the plane, another Amigo Squad member and I went into the cockpit and took pictures of ourselves sitting in the pilot's seat. We were giggling like schoolgirls. The search team was prepared to dismantle the interior of the fuselage all the way down to metal, but that hardly proved necessary: every unclaimed space was stuffed with bales of pot and bricks of coke—behind panels in the passenger compartments, above the false ceiling in the bathrooms, underneath the carpet in storage holds. Anything that was plastic came off, and behind that were drugs, waiting to be offloaded by ground crews as soon as all airline personnel left the plane. Both the baggage handlers and the cleaning crews left the airport through the employee exit, and airport security was none the wiser.

Air Cannabis, we called it.

Another offshoot of the Amigo Squad took us to Puerto Rico. This was much later. It was the brainchild of Rod Carscallen, my handler on Project Horseshoe who met me at Cherry Beach when they called off the Italian job the first time. Rod was fifteen years older than we were and served as a mentor and role model for Scotty, Robo and, quite frankly, all of us. Just pound for pound the greatest natural-born policeman I've ever encountered. He was a team leader, and he had contacts everywhere because everyone liked him. I would describe him as unimpeachable. He was always ten steps ahead of other policemen and of police culture in general. If word suddenly came down that Pablo Escobar was the head of the Medellin Cartel, Rod would have had him on his radar for a decade and have a network of informants already in place. He had guys all over the world—he was like a one-man intelligence service; he looked like a tiny Santa Claus, and you just wanted to sit on his knee and tell him everything. There were so many times when he would file reports that the division heads either didn't read or couldn't grasp, things that came to pass far after the fact. I can't say enough about the guy. He died in 2004, far too young at fifty-two. I delivered the eulogy at his funeral.

Rod came to Scotty and me and said, "Boy, have I got something for you two. Maybe you guys can do something with it." He had an informant in the Medellin Cartel who was willing to give up all their drug-trafficking routes for the entire country of Canada. We got it approved by headquarters, and Scotty and I flew to San Juan, Puerto Rico—a logical place to rendezvous, since the Mall of the Americas was a famous shopping destination for Colombians. We checked into our hotel and decided to take a long walk down the beach to a cabana bar, where we had to hop a chain to get a drink. The next day we met the informant's FBI and DEA handlers to lay down some ground rules for the interview, and one of them said, "Just so you guys know—never, ever walk down the beach away from the hotel. They have three or four decapitations a night along that stretch."

We met the informant in a hotel suite—the U.S. feds in their suits and us in our shorts and flip-flops. We also brought a big jug of vodka and pineapple juice along with us, just in case. Everyone turned on tape recorders and we started chatting with the informant, because when you chat, stuff comes out. But one of the suits said, "Please state your question." The question would be something like, "What was your most popular route this week? What about last week?" Then the FBI guy would repeat the question, they'd shut off the tape recorder, and there would be a thirty-second whisper session about whether they were going to let him answer. This was going nowhere. We got to about three-thirty or four in the afternoon and the FBI guy said, "That's enough for today." As we were all shuffling out, Scotty whispered our room number to the informant.

At nine that evening there was a knock at the door. It was the informant, who told us, "I had to lose those fucking guys. You got anything to drink?" In fact we did: our big jug of vodka and pineapple juice, barely dented. At 5 a.m., we were still talking a mile a minute; he gave us everything. We were supposed to meet the Feds again at 9 a.m., so we finally called it a night. The next morning Scotty and I had to pretend we had no idea what he was talking about.

A year into my assignment in Toronto I got a call from a guy named Andy Mayo in the Amigo Squad who had replaced me after one of my periodic stints there. He said, "I just got the strangest phone call. Some guy from Montreal named Gabé called and asked for you. I told him you weren't here right now but that I could take a message. He says to call him."

Holy fuck! Andy Mayo wasn't an undercover, and he was certainly not a confidant who would have known my prior plays. He was just the guy they assigned my old cell-phone number to, and he had the presence of mind in the moment to keep my subterfuge alive. Nice work.

I phoned Gabé back and he said, "Okay, Bob, we're ready to go ahead. I'll fax you the waybills and everything you need." He laid out the scope of the operation they had planned, how much they wanted to pay, how often the ship-ments would arrive—a wealth of logistical information. I already had a day job (one that ostensibly precluded under-cover work), but there was no way to turn this down.

The Amigo Squad jumped at it. I already had an import-export business all worked out; I just had to pull the trigger. The first bill of lading arrived for a container coming in on a flight from India. We met the plane like the cavalry. The whole thing came off like clockwork, and then . . . the container was empty. Gabé called and said, "You get the container?"

I said, "Yeah, there's nothing in it."

"Yeah, right. Fuck off."

"No, really. There's nothing in it."

When he understood I wasn't kidding, Gabé got testy on the phone and hung up. It was the first sign of emotion I'd seem him show, and it was a little spooky. He hung up a couple of times before I could convince him that I was telling the truth. Either he sent the first one as a trial run, or else one of his henchmen did and didn't bother to tell him. Finally it ironed itself out and we made plans to try it again. And once more, when the container arrived, it turned out to be a dry run. And again. And again. It got to where my Amigo pals were sick of running out to Pearson and pulling containers off planes full of everything but drugs.

Finally, on the seventh try, there was a half-ton of hash on board—483 kilos. The plan was that I would rent a Ryder truck and transport the shipment to Montreal and await their instructions. This was to be a controlled delivery, where you open the shipping container, remove the dope, replace it with something of equal weight and texture and then repackage everything exactly the way it was and ship it on to the intended recipient.

In this case the hash was wrapped in cellophane, coated with cayenne pepper, curry spice and mustard (to throw off drug-sniffing dogs), heat-sealed in plastic, then wrapped in Persian rugs. A Canada Customs bloodhound hit it walking by the container. In addition, the bales of hash were sewn together in a hand-stitched material a little finer than burlap, in the manner of commercial shipments from Pakistan. Which meant that if we replaced the hash by weight with sand, we had to replace the stitching as well. Amigo boss Billy Henderson located six elderly seamstresses in the garment district who were familiar with this technique and could replicate it to keep the fiction intact. We reloaded the truck, and on the drive up, Gabé and his men were constantly on the phone tracking our progress, even while I was on hold with the Sûreté du Québec, trying to coordinate the takedown, since we had no jurisdiction in their region. Once I arrived, Gabé gave me directions to a dead-end street in the abandoned warehouse section down by the Old Port of Montreal. I told them no way and picked the middle of a Walmart parking lot in Laval for the safety of wide-open spaces. Your money for the keys to my truck.

After we settled the details they showed up with big bundles of money. I had done a lot of drug deals, but this looked like something right out of *The French Connection*: cubes of bills sealed in Ziploc baggies, with a freezer smell, and mouldy, as if it had been buried in dirt. But it was money, so I took it. When they opened the back of the Ryder truck, the ninjas rocked their world. We were told later by the Montreal police that the money came from a city bank robbery maybe twenty years before—old enough that the currency was a different design—and they had just been saving it for a rainy day. So we got them on that too. Nick Pron, a crime reporter for the *Toronto Star*, got wind of the story and filed a piece ten days later about what was then the largest drug deal in Canadian history (thankfully leaving my UC role out of it).

The postscript to that story is that the people they imported the hash from decided they had a rat, since everyone else went down. And the guy they suspected was not me but some hapless schlub somewhere in the supply chain who had managed to elude arrest. They dragged him out of his Montreal condo one morning in his underwear, doused him with gasoline and set him on fire, then shot him, just to be safe. The first any of us heard about it was the Nick Pron story in the Sunday paper. I got on the phone to Smitty and he got on the phone to White, and we all read the article, speechless.

CHAPTER 10

THE RUSSIANS ARE COMING

By 1997, I'd been promoted to staff sergeant in charge of the Toronto Drug Unit. I got a call from Tromper, the grizzled supervisor at CFSEU who flagged me on to Vegas while I was tailing Eddie Melo on the Italian organized crime detail. The world of proven, available UCs in the OPP was very limited, so they kept tapping the same guys over and over again to be their Uncle Charlie—even guys like me who had supposedly sworn off the life. Just as John White did with the King of Morocco, Tromper said, "Bob, we need a guy to go in once, maybe twice a month tops, and meet with Russian organized crime. It's a heat-seeking mission; just see if you can get a feel for what's going on with them."

I knew that this job, like so many others, had the potential to spin out into something way more involved than a couple of brief monthly check-ins. Tromper was fully aware that I wasn't likely to pass on the opportunity. Knowing the ins and outs of my CV, he remembered that when I was in high school I had worked part-time at Birks, the jewellery store, repairing watches and broken necklace clasps and ring settings. He used that prior experience as a pretext to get me assigned to a major undercover jewellery-smuggling ring, then sent me to the largest gold-and-diamond wholesale operation in central Canada, run by Russian mobsters.

An agent was supposed to walk me into their flagship operation in downtown Toronto and introduce me to the crime family who ran it. We met a couple of times and practiced our story until it was airtight; he stood to pull down a sizable payday for his services. On the day of the meet, we went to the high-security two-storey building and walked down a long flight of concrete stairs to below street level. They buzzed us into a small holding chamber where they could study us on video as the first door locked behind us, and then buzzed us through the second door inside. It was like entering prison. Other parts of the building housed floor-to-ceiling safes, diamond-cutting machines and a workshop where Russian immigrants assembled jewellery parts—all watched over by ever-present security cameras.

When we entered the jewellery showroom I noticed a profound change come over the agent. Gone was the suave confidant of master criminals and glib architect of his own deceptions—I could see his confidence diminishing with each step. He was visibly trembling.

Behind the counter was the patriarch of Russian organized crime in Canada. Recognizing the agent, he motioned with his head that we should step into the adjacent office. When we entered, a man in a dark suit was sitting behind a massive desk. The agent unceremoniously muttered, "Rob, this is Sam—you guys should talk." Without another word he turned and bolted. This was my formal introduction to the Russian mafia.

I was now face to face with a man who headed both legitimate and illegitimate enterprises, whose time was valuable and who placed zero value on the virtue of strangers. Suddenly he saw my cake-hole gawping at him inside his inner sanctum.

"The fuck you want?" he snarled.

I was pretty sure we couldn't reschedule. So I sprinkled a little sand on the floor and gave him the old soft shoe. I told him, "My name is Rob and I'm here to solve your problems. Give me three minutes to tell you how." I took a deep breath and motored through on high-octane adrenalin alone, speed-walking up and down every last aisle in my mind, upselling every resource I could marshal to offer him. When I got to a stand-alone, off-the-shelf import-export business, I saw his eyes narrow. I didn't stop for the whole three minutes, and by the time I was done I was out of breath.

My audition went well, but it was only the first step in a many-months-long process of infiltration and trust building.

Our relationship began with me making frequent use of their money-laundering services, one of their many areas of expertise. The police had never had a UC inside the Russian mob before, and the possibilities were open-ended. We just had to be patient.

Eventually, just as had happened with the Italians, I was accompanying these guys everywhere they went. The family comprised a father and his three sons—the smart one, the brawny one and the quiet one. It was just like *The Godfather*.

The brother I'll call Adam was the youngest and the smartest, and he's who I spent 90 percent of my time with. He even ended up naming one of his children Robert, and I suspected I might have been some influence on that. He looked like a young Al Pacino. Daniel was the middle son, a muscle-bound hothead who was way into crime, and who would just as soon kill you as look at you. Jacob, the oldest and the quietest, knew everything there was to know about diamonds, so you had to listen to him.

What all three sons had in common was that they lived in fear of their father. Fat and beefy, never smiling, with eyes that burned straight through you, he reminded me of a bloodless, sadistic Ed Asner. The parents had emigrated from Russia through Israel to Toronto, and the three boys grew up in the world of organized crime, so it was all they ever knew. They were extremely rich, and all lived in separate houses on the same circular cul-de-sac that functioned as a private compound. They were the most selfish people I'd ever met in my twenty years of socializing with sociopaths and murderers.

Everything revolved around information, political influence and leverage. They dressed in full Versace, from underwear to overcoat, and always paid for everything in cash. We would eat at the most fashionable restaurants in Toronto, where dinner for four of us routinely topped $5,000, and they would be rude to the waiters. Who is rude to waiters? You were constantly being embarrassed when you were out with them. They decided they wanted to learn to play golf and sent me out to buy top-dollar clubs and equipment. Then once we got to the course, they raced golf carts and tore up the greens, then yelled, "What are you looking at?" at anyone who stared at them. Women were like chattel to them, little more than slaves. The only woman I ever saw them show respect to was their mother, but that just might have been so their father didn't kill them.

It was about a year into my assignment when Adam brought up my import-export business. He wanted to know all about it, especially about my man on the inside at Customs. I knew then that he was hooked and cooked. He explained to me the way the smuggling world worked at that level: if you're smuggling something for me, and it's worth $400,000, I will tell you everything you need to know to go and get it. In exchange you will give me $400,000 to hold. If you die or don't show back up, I'm paid. If I get cashiered while you're away, you've got the diamonds. If you do show back up and I'm still here, I'll give you your money back plus a 10 percent smuggler's fee in return for the contraband. It completely takes the risk out of the business. If I could show them some-thing and make it work, we could do business.

I took this back to my superiors and they said no, abso-lutely not. It was too rich for their blood—even when I explained that they would get their money back and then some. The word that came down from Accounting was, "See if you can get them to do it without the money."

The joke was on me, because they said yes. Adam was so impressed with me and liked me so much that he spotted me the money. I explained to the Russians how my import-export business operated, and that they would control their merchandise right up until we actually moved it through Customs. Since the border crossing was fixed, there was minimal risk to spread between us. So they went for it.

We titled it Project Oprava, which allegedly means "to repair or correct" in Russian, since the division of the RCMP we were partnered with insisted that all their projects begin with the letter O. (Hey, you try it.) We did the first shipment, which was gold from Italy, as a kind of test. It turns out that the Italian government is extremely vigilant about its export protocols and paperwork—who knew?—so I had to legally ship the gold to Switzerland first, then smuggle it to myself at Pearson utilizing the system I had perfected for the King of Morocco. After the first instalment went off without a catch I quickly became their in-house smuggler. Because there were still deals in the pipeline, we sent some of our early shipments to the U.S. and drove them across the border. Diamonds, their other mainstay, were mainly raw ones from

South Africa that came in little white envelopes, which we also rerouted through Switzerland. And it made a big difference whether the gold or diamond products were store-ready or still to be processed (labelled "parts")—e.g., necklaces with the clasps enclosed in a separate box. Restrictions on parts were far more lenient.

Like the Italians, they were into any exotic breed of crime, as long as it promised a return on their investment of money and time. While I was there they floated phony IPOs on the Vancouver Stock Exchange. Once I was present at a meeting where they brokered a truce between the Satan's Choice and Para-Dice Riders motorcycle clubs. It may not have been as sexy as the coke trade, but there was always a lot of money. (For one thing, when you're smuggling gold and diamonds, you're saving 33 percent in taxes right off the top, enabling you to mercilessly undercut the competition.)

Soon our meetings moved to Adam's house. It was located in a gated neighbourhood, one of these monstrosities with hand-carved marble steps and surveillance cameras everywhere. Their foyer was the size of a small auditorium and produced its own echo.

One evening I decided to pop in to Adam's mansion with a personal gift: a PalmPilot, the era's gadget of choice. It was supposed to be a brief visit and I was with a couple of cover men, so they crouched down in the back seat of the car that was parked on the circular cobblestone driveway. Adam wasn't content to merely take delivery of his present—he insisted I come in and stay awhile. As Adam and I chatted about the features of his new toy, I happened to glance up at the bank of security cameras on the wall and, to my horror, witnessed one of the cover men exiting the car and taking a leak in the fountain in the centre of the driveway. Luckily he was a model of efficiency if not subterfuge.

Due to the nature of the family's business, we also travelled constantly—we'd go to New York, Miami and Orlando to meet with our international contacts and hammer out the details of deals as they arose. We always met at some kind of jewellers' convention—hence, Orlando. And I spent a lot of time in the hot tub with the Russians—on one especially memorable occasion at Walt Disney World, Adam and I indulged in $500 cigars while he shared with me his personal formula for succeeding as a criminal.

With access to organized crime again came the trappings of unearned success. My dad came to visit me once in Toronto when I was in the middle of the Russian job, and he was unnerved by all the conspicuous consumption. I drove a Mercedes, a Porsche and a Z3 BMW and ran my own import-export business, and he didn't want anything to do with any of it. He understood intellectually what I was doing, but to him every one of those things screamed drug dealer. I had to tone it way down and tell him to forget about all that. He never told his relatives in Ireland what I did—the undercover stuff—and he never talked about it with his mates. When my paternal grandfather died I was deep undercover with the Russians, and I couldn't attend the funeral in Ireland. My mom told me after my dad died that he had worried about me all the time.

One time when I was meeting Adam at his office there was a *Maclean's* magazine on his coffee table that had a picture of me in the Outlaw Motorcycle Gang Unit, standing at a biker party with a couple of Para-Dice Riders patches. He didn't recognize me from the photo, and I wasn't identified, but it was a wake-up call that maybe I shouldn't be doing undercover work, having by this point appeared in newspapers, now magazines and on television. I slipped the issue under the Dolce & Gabbana coffee-table book just to be safe.

At some point early in our two-year arc, since I was constantly over at Adam's house and around his wife and family, it became a point of contention that they had never met anyone in my life—specifically, a girlfriend. I assured them I had an active social life, but eventually the situation was like dating someone and now it was time to bring her home to meet your parents. There was a big Christmas party coming up, the Versace Ball, and I was expected to bring someone. If I didn't, it would have looked suspicious.

There's obviously a big distinction in Canadian law enforcement between Special Services, which is the umbrella term for all the drug, surveillance and intelligence units, and everyone else who's in uniform. For that reason most of us in the Flying Squad who had been around awhile made ourselves available to lecture at the various police academies and colleges, both as a recruiting tool for undercover work and just to educate rank-and-file police officers on the view from the bleeding edge, especially when it came to drugs, bikers and other institutional crime. Anyone can memorize the criminal statutes, but assimilating a criminal lifestyle is a little trickier, and you have a finite number of chances to fuck up. At a training seminar on bikers, I was lecturing uniform members from the region on the rules of engagement—if you pull someone over and they're flying colours, what you need to know. They had rented a small auditorium, and halfway through my talk a striking woman in uniform came in who made an impression on me. At the end I was passing out handouts but there weren't enough, so I asked if someone from each detachment could take one and make copies for the rest. She raised her hand and said, "I'm from Caledon," meaning she was happy to volunteer for her group. But it came off as adorably dorky, and I said, "How nice for you," or something equally smartass. Everyone laughed, and she turned beet red. I got her name on the stairs walking out—Lorra—and we talked for a while afterwards. Then, being a cop, I found out everything I could about her as soon as I got to a computer—five years on the force, well liked, no red flags. She was twenty-nine—seven years younger than I was.

Since the Christmas party was coming up, my cover team was allegedly working overtime to get me a date. We used to have a saying that the OPP hired women by the pound, and when they trotted out a couple of prospective arm-pieces culled for me from the ranks, it was clearly not going to work. Competent policewomen all of them no doubt, but they were not going to enhance my status as the golden boy in my new Russian family. These guys all had Russian-model girlfriends or china-doll wives, and my escort was going to have to survive in that snakepit.

Not long afterwards I went to a takedown party for a Toronto Drugs project I had been a part of, held in Barrie. Lorra had tagged along with a friend of hers who knew our whole crowd going way back, and I ran into the two of them at the bar. I kept buying them drinks, and the more Lorra drank, the more she blossomed. On a whim I told her about the Versace Ball, and that I needed a police escort. This was four or five drinks in, and she thought I was out of my mind. But then I put in a formal request through her detachment, and she had to consider it seriously. She seemed to think this was some elaborate seduction on my part, and that her career would be damaged accordingly, but I gave her the breakdown of who the players were and what was at stake. I managed to impress on her that while it might sound like fun, it was going to be hard work and very stressful. She seemed to have an immediate grasp of the situation and agreed to do it.

The night of the Versace Ball we were both dressed to the nines: I was wearing a $5,000 suit and she looked like a million bucks. And she did unbelievably well. The men all drooled over her, and the wives thought she was sweet. We sat on the dais with the family, and she and I were the envy of everyone. We stayed through the dinner, the reception and the first part of the dance, and then we faded into the woodwork. First rule of UC work: get out before anything can go wrong—whether it's a drug deal or a black-tie gala. For her, the whole thing was like a James Bond movie. She also had a flair for it. From there on out, whenever I needed to flash my girlfriend, she was on call. In retrospect, it turned out to be a perfect first date, since it took all the romantic pressure off us and replaced it with actual danger.

When we had an opening in the drug unit, I made the argument to my superiors that it was about time we started to cultivate female undercover agents. It was an unassailable argument, albeit one that looks padded with ulterior motives. So sue me. She was skeptical at first, but I brought her along to one of our training sessions, and during a break in the action I walked her outside to have a talk.

I told her, "The only reason you're here is because you're a good cop and everybody has only good things to say about you. You did great on your trial run, and from where I sit you're the best candidate for the job. None of that will change. However, I should probably tell you that I like you, and I did from the first time I saw you. So there's that." She didn't act as though what I'd said to her would pose any problems. While I was off doing all the other stuff I had to do, she did two undercover projects on her own as part of a cover team in the drug squad and made a name for herself. More than a year after that we were dating fast and furious and keeping it a secret from everyone we knew. She was living undercover *twice removed*.

After my ex-wife left Toronto with the kids, Lorra and I finally went public. She's still a cop, and today we're married with three kids of our own.

———

I spent two years, give or take, with the Russians, running their import-export operation, and the patriarch couldn't have been happier with me. Of course, he would never show it, and I had to hear about it from his eldest son. I got word that we were going to Miami—as always our trip took place under the pretext of an international jewellery convention, this one at the Convention Center in Orlando. I flew down there with Adam and some of his bodyguards— me, Tom Hagen, the Irish consigliere to his Russian Michael Corleone. The night before at the hotel, Adam decided he would hit the convention centre early the next morning, where he had scheduled a number of meetings. Since I didn't need to be there for any of those, I decided to sleep in—in reality, the perfect pretext to check in with my cover team and download some of my intel. I would rendezvous with him for lunch afterwards at an outdoor café near the convention centre.

After I had met with the cover team and done my notes and debriefing, they dropped me off near the convention centre and went to find a place to park where they could observe the goings-on. I picked a spot on the corner near the café to wait, since the Russians were always late. While I was standing there, my Spidey sense started to tingle, and I noticed what looked like a set-up unfolding around me. I watched as plainclothes police rolled in on all four corners, not doing a terribly good job of concealing themselves, and a surveillance car hovered nearby in heavy traffic. I thought to myself,

Something is about to go down and I'm going to have a front-row seat for it—this is excellent! All I had to do was wait. Out of my peripheral vision I noticed a guy walking up the street toward me who also looked like a plainclothes cop. I thought maybe something had happened with the cover team and these guys were the cavalry.

He said, "Excuse me, sir."

I turned to face him and said, "Yes?" and then BOOM—I was taken down from behind. Uniformed cops had me on the ground and were cuffing me. They emptied my pockets, got my jacket and passport—which was in the name of my cover identity, of course—while a small army of Orlando's finest descended on the street corner. They bundled me into the back of a black-and-white, and as we pulled into traffic I watched the cops back on the street high-fiving and saying, "We got the fucker!" When I tried to ask the two city cops in the squad car who they thought they had, they invited me to shut the fuck up.

On one hand I still felt as if I had the best seat at the show, since this was obviously a case of mistaken identity. But that was quickly being overtaken by a rising panic. My cover team was still no more than blocks away, and they were extremely resourceful, but they also were limited as to what they could say to others. The prime directive for a UC is the same as for an actor: never, ever break character. For all I knew, Orlando PD had a rogue element that was wired straight into the Russian mob. This was Florida, after all. Plus, from what I had seen of Central Florida's finest, they had acted like buffoons from start to finish—behaviour that did not inspire confidence. If I hadn't already, I suddenly understood why people hate cops: they do not listen. Once they make up their minds, you cannot get them off the dime.

They put me in a cell at the nearest precinct; up to this point, no one had explained to me what I was doing there. They fingerprinted me, put me in a photo lineup (even though I was the only one in line) and finally ushered me into a small interview room with a table and two chairs. This all took several hours, and by then I could hear the voices of the Russians right outside. Did they execute the takedown without me? Did my cover get blown and they had to move without letting me know? The detective who had finger-printed me unlocked the door and motioned for me to follow him. I could see the whole family amassed on the other side of the booking desk. Then suddenly they gave me my pos-sessions back and released me. The Russians grabbed me and hustled me out of the police station as if they'd just won the hundred-yard dash. Down the marble steps in front, and then hugs and kisses all around once we were back on the street.

They brought me up to speed. Running late as usual, they had showed up at the café just after noon and couldn't find any sign of me. Some other patrons of the café said, "Are you looking for your friend? I think the police got him."

Not understanding the big picture any better than I did, the Russians stopped the first cop they could find and asked him, "If my friend got arrested on that street corner over there, where would they take him?" The cop refused to tell them, so they got on a pay phone and started calling precincts. Since I hadn't been booked yet, there was no record of my incarceration, so Adam just kept phoning until he finally found where I was being held. City police had mistaken me for an international diamond-and-jewel thief who was on the FBI's Top Ten Most Wanted list, due to a vague physical similarity, combined with the fact that I was loitering outside a huge international gold-and-diamond convention, which they took as motive. Since the police had no hard evidence, and the Russians were very aggressive about threatening legal repercussions, they let me go. As soon as we were clear of the police station, Adam called everybody up the food chain in reverse order, each time playing up how I had refused to break cover. His father was quick to relay the story to some mafia associates in Brighton Beach, the Brooklyn home of the Russian mob, I went from being deep inside the Russian mafia to deep, deep inside; it was the closest my Irish ass was ever going to get to becoming a made man.

Months later I rescheduled with their contact at the Federal Reserve Building and travelled to Miami, this time alone—just me and my RCMP cover guy following at a discreet distance. The Russians had a standing arrangement with the contact, and now that I was a hero they were going to let me handle both ends of the deal: I would organize the shipment of gold and diamonds to him at the Federal Reserve Building, and then instead of using a runner I would pick it up and smuggle it back to Toronto personally. Since I had handled shipments of this magnitude before, it seemed like a

200 | BOB DEASY

cakewalk. And since this meeting also involved the exchange of illegal goods, the decision was made on our end to use it to light the fuse on the takedown. Since I would be on U.S. soil, the FBI would provide liaison, as the U.S. equivalent of the RCMP. I went to the Federal Reserve Building armed with a duffel bag, walked into the cover man's giant safe and loaded it up with all the gold and diamonds I could carry. Then I walked out of the building, avoiding the scanners altogether—no one stopped me—and directly to my cover man's car in the parking lot, where he drove me to a rendezvous with the Feds. Two FBI agents escorted me to the airport and through security, in case a bag full of gold and uncut diamonds were to raise anyone's suspicions. With them watching me, I set my army-surplus knapsack on the conveyor belt and watched as no one even looked twice. The FBI guys just rolled their eyes.

Since it was unclear what the immediate threat to me would be, it was decided that the takedown back in Toronto should take place while I was still in the air. This takedown wouldn't nab just the Russians but all their smuggling contacts around the world. Through the CFSEU's contacts at Interpol, we coordinated with the relevant law enforcement agencies in each of the host countries—the United States, Italy, Switzerland, Austria and so on. On the three-hour flight from Miami to Toronto, while the outside world I had been immersed in for the past two years was undergoing a seismic breach, with several million dollars' worth of precious metal and compressed carbon in the carry-on bag at my feet,

I had time to reflect on the universe and my place in it. I was relieved, the way I always am at the end of a project, the steady flow of adrenalin finally staunched to provide a much-needed respite. But this time there was something else—a feeling of "what now"? Double or nothing to infinity is not a good game plan. There was nothing up there above me but the roof of the world—I could see it from where I was sitting—and even if I managed to climb on top of it, the prospect seemed infinitely lonely.

When I touched down at Pearson, a bank of flashing red lights appeared on the tarmac. Everyone on board looked at one another with alarm, probably thinking it was the bomb squad or something. And who knows what they thought when I stood up and was escorted off the plane. Since there was a possibility I could have a price on my head, I had to lie down in the back of one of the police SUVs as we proceeded a short distance to a hotel near the airport, where I completed my debriefing and the last of my project notes.

Generally, at the end of a project, if an Uncle Charlie has successfully infiltrated them and brought them down from the inside, a criminal organization is more interested in coming after the informant—the agent who first vouched for the UC and walked him inside. Over the long term this is a more efficient means of quality control: it's the agent who betrayed the enterprise. The cop was just doing his job. But this time was different. The damage wrought was on an international scale. I had been a surrogate member of their family. And they had also risked major exposure to get me

202 | BOB DEASY

out of jail in Orlando. It felt a lot more personal, and there was no way to tell how far they would go to exact revenge. After the Russians had their day in court and everyone had been tagged and bagged, Tromper went to the Russian patriarch's lawyer and said, "All's fair in love and war. Tell your guy if he moves against any of my men, he will rue the day." Or at least that's what he told me he said.

CHAPTER 11

OUTLAW BIKERS

For people who don't live in Canada, it's hard to convey the significance of outlaw biker gangs and the criminal influence they exert here. In the States, for instance, where the one-percenter clubs started in California after the Second World War, they're defined in the popular imagination by Brando in the *The Wild One* or Jack Nicholson in *The Rebel Rousers* or *Hells Angels on Wheels*. They're still portrayed in movies and TV—often for comic effect nowadays—as thugs and dead-enders, subliterate nomads who travel in packs and live beyond the reach of laws and civilization, largely by choice. This isn't exactly the persona we see in Canada. A biker gang like the Hells Angels—variously known as HA or the Big Red Machine here—which absorbed its competition at the turn of the millennium as ruthlessly as the Wehrmacht at full throttle, is quite possibly the most efficient criminal organization in the history of the world. They get others to commit crimes for them, and they are insulated through their viciousness and intense loyalty in a way that the Italians or Russians never were. Their presence in Canada is ubiquitous, which means that they show up in almost every project I've ever been a part of.

I went head-to-head with them twice, both times as a member of a special SSG or Special Support Group (or, alternatively, the Provincial Special Squad), which internally we referred to colloquially as the Bike Squad. The first time was between 1995 and 1997, when I was sergeant. The second time was after we did the Russians, during the dreaded Biker Wars in Quebec, when I returned as staff sergeant and we ran Project Turmoil against the Hells Angels, who were in the midst of a hostile takeover of rogue biker gangs throughout Ontario.

The original Bike Squad consisted of four full-time OPP case officers. When I joined, the other three were Lenny, George and Doug, whom we called Fluf, which stood for Fat Little Ugly Fucker. The bikers loved him because he looked like a lethal fireplug. Every local police force in Ontario where there was a biker chapter had one officer who was part-time on the SSG—they were our designated official liaisons, so we always had a man in the field wherever we needed one. And it worked both ways—they'd keep us in the loop on what was going down in their regions and call us in as needed.

Our focus was primarily intelligence gathering. Since there were only four of us, we didn't organize ourselves into formal projects. Instead, each of us took a separate MC (motorcycle club) and made it our specialty: Fluf had the Outlaws, Lenny had Satan's Choice, George took the Vagabonds and mine was the Para-Dice Riders. As a loose coalition these groups proved daunting enough to keep the Hells Angels from gaining a foothold in Ontario until the late '90s. This situation was maintained until the Big Red Machine ran out of other territories to eat for breakfast.

Everybody I know in the Flying Squad and throughout the UC subculture has had a similar experience. Robo worked the Satan's Choice in the York region in Project Dismantle, where he bought so many stolen cars that a barn had to be rented just to keep them all out of sight. Scotty spent four years in the Bike Squad working UC projects on the Outlaws and the Iron Wings, as well as Project Overhaul, which targeted the Oshawa and East Toronto chapters of the Satan's Choice before they joined with the HA. We're all among the select few who ever made hand-to-hand deals with patch-wearing gang members. Smitty did Project Bandito and Project Disarm, both biker projects. They were just too ubiquitous not to rub up against once in a while.

I made no secret of my interest in the Para-Dice Riders. When the gang had church meetings—their weekly assembly, every Wednesday evening—I was parked in front of the clubhouse taking down licence plate numbers and greeting members as they arrived. When they went on the road I went with them, following at a respectable distance. This activity was all conducted out in the open, and they knew me by name and considered me a mascot of sorts. It got to the point that if I didn't show up on church night they would get suspicious and think something was up. It was the same with the other squad members and their assigned clubs. I'm sure the bikers felt validated by the attention. Of course, this was as much for show as anything else. A constable walking a beat will get to know his constituency, even the part that falls within the criminal element. Pretty soon that becomes a two-way street. At the same time, we were gathering intelligence on the other six days just the same as on any other project or case.

This slow and steady collection of intel changed overnight as a consequence of the open Biker Wars between the Hells Angels and the Rock Machine, an entrenched MC based in the province of Quebec. After several highly publicized incidents—including a car bombing that claimed the life of eleven-year-old Daniel Desrochers—and a body count that eventually reached 150, public sentiment demanded action, and Queen's Park increased Bike Squad personnel from four to sixty with the stroke of a pen, and raised its budget to $8 million, rebranding it the Outlaw Motorcycle Gang Unit. Whereas before we had been den mothers shepherding data between the requirements of our day jobs, now the Bike Squad became a permanent assignment, with a host of elaborate projects designed to dismantle the biker infrastructure in Ontario.

The Hells Angels victory in the turf wars in Quebec, centring on Montreal, emboldened them to take another run at the loose consortium of rogue clubs that dominated Ontario. This culminated in the Patch Over, a consolidation of rival biker gangs under the Hells Angels banner. Clubs like the Satan's Choice, the Para-Dice Riders, the Loners and the Vagabonds, all of whom were sworn enemies of the HA, were given the opportunity to retire their club patches and replace them with the legendary red-and-white death's-head-and-angel's-wing logo and the prestige and power it represented. Each chapter of every club had to vote individually, and the debate was intense. Hanging in the balance was a virtual civil war that threatened to overshadow the bloodshed in Quebec. Finally, on New Year's Eve 2000, technically the last night before the onset of the new millennium, the Patch Over took place simultaneously all across Ontario, and on the morning after there were seven new Ontario chapters of the Hells Angels.

The Patch Over was largely the brainchild of one man—Walter (Nurget) Stadnick, a diminutive Hamilton brawler with burn marks on his face and arms from a long-ago motorcycle wreck. Stadnick was notorious for having formed the Nomads, a non-region-specific chapter of the Hells Angels that had no turf to defend and so was free to operate anywhere in North America with impunity. Someone like Sonny Barger, president of the Angels' chapter in Oakland, California, in the 1960s, might seem like a poster child for the HA on the strength of his profile in Hunter

Thompson's *Hell's Angels: The Strange and Terrible Saga of the Outlaw Motorcycle Gangs*, as well as his oversight of security at the Rolling Stones concert at Altamont Speedway in 1969, during which the Angels administered numerous savage beatings and murdered a man in front of the stage (captured on camera in the documentary *Gimme Shelter*). And yet both his legacy and place in the group's international hierarchy would fall far short of Stadnick, a galvanizing figure whose strategic vision matched the Angels' elite identity with a secure power base and financial windfall. Free to cross provincial borders with abandon, Stadnick saw his influence as the head of the Nomads quickly grow to rival that of Maurice (Mom) Boucher, head of the Montreal chapter, where the club had established its national headquarters. Mom Boucher presided over a monthly meeting in Montreal called La Table that included the Italians, the Asians and every other criminal entity of consequence, at which they set a price for drugs, prostitution, extortionate interest rates and all other financial aspects of their business. Unfettered by official boundaries, they quickly became the Hells Angels' ambassadors to the farthest reaches of its empire, as well as a dozen-man elite unit comparable to the marines—or the Flying Squad. By using a combination of the Hollywood glamour of the Hells Angels' name and the implicit intimidation of its enduring legacy, Stadnick was successful in taking the patchwork quilt of Ontario biker gangs and creating a unified criminal network—and with far less violence than was commonplace in Quebec.

The largest one-percenter motorcycle club in the world, the HA had always been bound by its shared history and intense loyalty. At the executive level there was virtually no way for an outsider to penetrate. It would take someone on the inside who was willing to flip—motivated by greed, caught in a vise and willing to leverage himself out of it or harbouring a world-class grudge. Luckily the Patch Over provided plenty of opportunity for all three.

The night the Para-Dice Riders voted to become Hells Angels and retire the patch, a lot of lifers came out of that meeting saying, "No fucking way. I've been a Para-Dice Rider for thirty years. I ain't an HA." George followed a bunch of them en masse to the HA chapter clubhouse in Sherbrooke, about 150 kilometres east of Montreal. They had rented buses, and people were pouring in from all across Ontario. It was like a papal conclave, waiting for the white smoke. Anyone who wanted to was welcome to wear the HA patch, but the clubs themselves would have to dissolve, and a lot of veterans retired that night—some of them less than amicably. But some of the old-timers knew what we had learned from watching the Big Red Machine spread across Canada like a giant welt: their charity was less than met the eye. These guys prided themselves on being the crème de la crème, and a lot of long-term members in the subordinate clubs would never have made the cut. The HA believed they could ultimately cherry-pick the members they wanted, and the ones who were too stupid or crazy to qualify they had ways of weeding out. The problem would take care of itself.

One of the dyed-in-the-wool Para-Dice Riders was a guy we'll call 4500. That was his agent number, and we could place him firmly in the grudge category. He argued long and loudly that giving up their charter and legacy was a terrible idea. In an era of forced mergers, hostile takeovers and predatory capitalism, conceding your position to real-life predators was not going to go any better. At that time he would have been forty, so he's sixty-something now. Been a biker his whole life, and he tried to tell the younger guys they had no idea what they were in for; once the HA rolls in, it's all about them and not about you. Suddenly you're working for Exxon or General Motors or any other global corporate leviathan that will consider you a resource to exploit to better its cumulative lot. For his trouble, they had a secret meeting before the big Patch Over debate and voted him out of the club.

I had known 4500 since my days in Project Tornado, my first undercover assignment, and he'd gone down at the end of that and done serious prison time. More recently he knew me as the OPP cop assigned to his chapter, so I'd been a part of his life for twenty years. After his expulsion he got word to me that he wanted to meet in a hotel room in the early afternoon. When I got there we weren't like long-lost friends exactly, but we did do some catching up and exchanged notes on mutual acquaintances and the odd wrinkles of fate that can befall people in our lines of work. This was our first conversation in all that time that didn't feature handcuffs or court bailiffs or lawyers standing between us, and we took our time easing into the business at hand. I have made it a point over the course of my career never to gloat after a bust; if the dude's caught, there's really no need to rub it in, and it's certainly not going to get him any more time. I think if that carried any deferred benefit, it would be in a situation like this, when career criminals come back to find me, looking for a fair shake, though at this point I still had no idea why he'd contacted me, or what he had to offer.

He told me the entire story of the Patch Over and his sudden exile. Left unmentioned, but obvious to both of us, was that this was just the first shoe to drop. He held the keys to the kingdom, new owners or not, and there was every chance that anyone looking at his situation dispassionately—if not his cohorts, then certainly senior management looking to hedge its losses—would designate him a liability. He continued his life of crime without the protection of his club, thus ending up in and out of jail on various charges. And in fact he did get lumped up pretty good at one point—no doubt with the authorization of some of his former crew. George and I went to see him in the hospital and thought he looked like a jack-o'-lantern, with huge black eyes and his jaw wired shut.

His best play now looked to be 1-800-CALL-BOB.

By the time he stopped talking, it was dark out. We'd been at it for five hours—no booze, no breaks, a lot of cigarettes and a dossier's worth of intense, high-level operational detail. Some of it was him hyping his story—and how it was going to make me the new OPP golden boy. But this was a guy who had a map to where the bodies were buried—and in this instance that wasn't just an expression—so he didn't really need to sell me. We made a plan where and how to meet, and I went and hand-carried him through the bureaucracy. In his favour with the boys upstairs was the fact that he hadn't come in with a list of demands. To the contrary: he didn't want to sign up as a confidential informant because in his mind he wasn't a rat. Anything he did for us was an act of self-defence in a time of war, for which his prior actions had left him little choice. And any lump sum payment would stand in the way of his self-image. He preferred instead a negotiated settlement for every piece of information he provided—more a gratuity than blood money. We had a sense of what this stuff was worth in the drug world: ten keys of coke? That's a pretty good pinch. Here's five grand. Ten keys plus a homicide? Okay, that would be worth more. So eventually it found its own level. He was a man with his own kind of principle who had made a stand and suffered the consequences.

He knew how dope moved around the province, and he gave us a lot of stash houses, tonnage of dope and a large part of the infrastructure. Maybe most valuably he gave us the kind of procedural intelligence on coded behaviour that in the long run saved us years of investigation and effort: if you see Arty the Biker headed east on the 401, it means this. Why things work the way they work, especially if they're designed with subterfuge in mind. He was easily worth triple the money we spent on him. We did drug rips, disrupted shipment lines, busted major figures so they went away for a dozen years or more. We were knocking these guys off with some regularity. Clouds of misinformation were cleared away in one concentrated effort. And the process lifted up an enormous rock: everything that was wriggling underneath we were charged with getting rid of.

One reason high-level Hells Angels prosecutions are rare is that whenever possible they insulate themselves from the actual crimes they commit. We had some of them up on wires, and every time a high-level confidential agent gave us another bust, it came back in the chatter as "How did that fucking guy get stopped by police?" To move their dope they would put up notices on university bulletin boards saying, "Drive my car to Toronto," for which they would pay a modest fee. On the back end it was always some guy who claimed he got paid $100 to pick up the car and drop it somewhere. Nobody had any idea they were transporting contraband, or any contact with the transporters, so it was senseless to prosecute them. There were no criminals on either end of the crime. So we would get a call saying, "Green Chev, service centre, last exit before Toronto," and we'd go toss it, take out all the dope—always in the back seat, sewn into the upholstery—seal it back up and wait for someone to come pick it up, follow them, see who picked that up and hope it would eventually lead us to bikers.

I actually made a couple of attempts to get 4500 plugged into productive society—asked him if he had any marketable skills, offered to make introductions. For all the good he did us, it was still a no-win situation for him, with stacked odds that he'd wind up dead or just patching another club. In all fairness that was the only life he'd ever known, and he hadn't left it by choice. He had his crew, his strippers, his dealers, his muscle and everyone knew he had been a Para-Dice Rider. What was he going to do—go back to school? I did try to pass him on to several Special Squad members, but I would always hear back that it was a bust. There's a special chemistry that's key to any operation's success, and once you start improving on it, you can easily suck the life right out of it. But more probably, this time it didn't work out because by then I'd spent two years with him—any drop of useful intelligence had been wrung out of him because I'd already carved him up six ways to Sunday.

I still see him on occasion—unofficially. I ran into him on a homicide case. He's a relic, at least in my world, from the days when you got your best stuff from a guy you met out in back of the Dumpster.

If you work undercover drugs your life revolves around rats, and the sooner you know that, the more successful you'll be. You've got best friends ratting on each other, mothers ratting on sons, wives ratting on husbands, love and honour cast asunder. It's a sobering spectacle. It's also the best tool we've got to combat institutional crime. If there is a clear-cut example of the end justifying the means, this is probably it: loyalty and "honour" neutralized by the corruption underpinning them.

And so you find your allegiances where they lie. In fact, I would say that probably half of what you get from the best agents you can't use because it's so specific that it could only have come from one place. In order to protect your source you have to constantly remain vigilant so as not to inadvertently give him up. They have a saying in biker culture: "Three can keep a secret if two are dead." The gig becomes how to orchestrate a campaign without anyone being able to retrace your steps. Sometimes it means finding corroborating evidence, sometimes it's deflecting attention elsewhere, and all too often it requires sitting on information that would prove radioactive if it ever saw the light of day. In a good working relationship, where the agent doesn't censor himself because he trusts you to protect him, you hold his life in your hands. It's 3-D chess, but this time against yourself: if you can find holes in your defences, others won't be far behind.

There was an agent who I developed whose identity has never been revealed, and if it were known, he would almost certainly be a target of the Hells Angels, even at this late date. In fact, there is precious little I can tell you about him, other than that he exists.

One night while I was tasked to the Bike Squad, a guy called me on my private cell number and said, "Are you Bob?"

I said, "Yeah, who are you?"

"It doesn't matter," the voice said. "I've got to meet you. I don't even really know why I'm doing this. But it's going to change your life."

"I like my life the way it is. Come on, dude—give me something."

He gave me some names and coloured in some details that very few people would know, and even fewer civilians.

One of the names was Walter Stadnick. His information checked out, and over the course of the next two years he did everything he claimed he could and more. We turned some of that information over to the Quebec provincial authorities, where it helped bring down the HA leadership, including, ultimately, Stadnick himself. The agent's demands weren't even all that outrageous: he wanted $700,000, which is essentially two or three fair-size drug deals, complete immunity and his extended family relocated out of the country. For that he essentially gave us the entire Hells Angels organization on a platter. He told me, "I will never, ever meet another policeman. Only you."

Whenever we had our meetings it was always some ungodly hour of the night. What new information he'd gleaned from Stadnick he'd pass on to me. He might say something like, "It'll be going down at the Central Hotel Thursday at ten. It's eighty keys, and you should look for a gold Charger with mags."

Provincial police protocol is that no informant could be the responsibility of any single officer; he now had to have a handling officer, a relocation officer, a supervisory officer—even a confidentiality officer. By the time he was done, the guy would be on a first-name basis with everyone in HQ. I ran it by the unnamed agent, and his reaction was as succinct as it was pornographic. I must have had hundreds of meetings about this; it never stopped. "You want to play? Then pay me. If not, then you can fuck right off." In the end, he did concede to meet with one other officer besides me.

The OPP Bike Squad had grown measurably in size, due to the workload resulting from the Patch Over's effects on the entire landscape of the biker wars. We were in the middle of a joint force operation with the Sûreté du Québec, and I was asked to give over what I'd learned from the agent to one of their wiretaps. I categorically refused because I knew there was no way to safeguard the agent's identity. Later the head of the Bike Squad on a subsequent project ordered me to turn over current information about him, and again I wouldn't give him up. I was on my way out to Homicide, and there were a bunch of threats made, snide remarks, dirty looks, think-tank meetings I had to get up and walk out of. As politely as possible I told them I couldn't help them and to bring on whatever they planned to throw at me, because the second I opened up about him he was burned. I may have things on my conscience, but that's not one of them.

This standoff created another round of what were effectively policy changes: "Officers will only meet with confidential agents where there are at least two other persons present." "Agents will sign a receipt in exchange for all payments." "Agents will provide a signature card to be kept on file to verify signature." Fine, except that this agent I've just spent six months cultivating is gonna powder the first inkling he gets that you have plans for him, and then the whole thing is in the wind. For the most part, we complied, since the chances of getting fucked by your own people were far greater than getting fucked by bikers. But they went as far as putting surveillance teams on us, their most decorated officers. Here was corporate oversight in a nutshell: instead of concentrating on the product—the quality of our police work and the amount of drugs taken off the streets—they worried about subjugating and second-guessing their labour force, reallocating their resources and emphasis against us, a captive audience who knew we were being spun. It was madness.

That generation of the Hells Angels' Ontario and Quebec organization was finally dismantled in Project Printemps (a.k.a. Project Springtime), Project Jacques and probably others, which claimed Mom Boucher, Walter Stadnick and most of the executive leadership of that venerated brand. They had the best lawyers money could buy, who would routinely interrupt court proceedings by demanding their clients' right to a trial in English, as Canadian citizens, even though everyone arrested in Montreal, with the exception of Stadnick and his right-hand man, Donald Stockford, were native French speakers. To prosecute the case, the provincial government *built* an entire courthouse: the prisoners' dock was a remote concealed unit made of unbreakable glass, wired with video cameras and microphones so that everyone could see everyone else. They were kept in a separate wing that was walled off from the courtroom, and all access was through a sealed tunnel. When the prisoner testified, both arms and legs were chained to bolts in the floor. Judge, attorneys and court personnel were protected in their own high-security enclosure. It was like Fort Knox. Huge chunks of time were used up on motions filed against the layout, and the Supreme Court had to rule on whether video access to the proceedings was constitutional. The trial lasted a full year. But by that time my promotion had gone through—I had already jumped to Homicide.

CHAPTER 12

MR. BIG

The Russian undercover was by far the longest, hardest and most taxing assignment I had ever been on, and when it was over, everything seemed different. In a two-year span—1999 to 2000—my marriage had broken up and my father had died. It was the hardest concentrated period I've ever had to go through, and at the end of it I was forced to take an internal inventory.

Ever since police college and my days in Geraldton, I had always idolized the major-case inspectors. These were the people who ran the murder investigations and other important cases. Dope was great: it was a giant Easter egg hunt, and if you were any good at reading the lay of the land, the break of the green, you could always figure out where the goodies were hidden. But Homicide had an extra edge to it. You had to read people, intuit their impulses and emotions, know when they're bullshitting you, or when they want you to know something, even when they think they don't. If Drugs is a giant treasure map, and you're the prospector or the pirate, Homicide is a giant puzzle, crossword or jigsaw, a pattern to find in a field of random data, and for the people you're up against, the outcome usually means life or death. It's more cerebral, an intellectual exercise, even though you're dealing with people's basest urges and truest emotions. I was the staff sergeant in charge of Toronto Drugs, and the next rank up was inspector, which was what you needed to join the Criminal Investigation Branch (CIB). That position also might finally allow me the chance for a normal domestic life. So when I was selected and promoted in 2002, I became one of the youngest detective inspectors in the history of the CIB.

I was in my early forties, and it had taken a long road and a lot of miles to get here, but this was where I wanted to be. I was still living out of a suitcase for too long at a time, but at least I could be seen dining out in public once in a while, or tell people what I did for a living. If you've ever seen *The First 48*, that's it; that's what I did. The life of an investigator is often filled with punishing, quotidian detail—like counting grains of sand, and makes about as much sense—and then all of a sudden something clicks: a car you saw on a surveillance tape eleven months ago shows up in a police file; an obscure nickname gets a hit in a database,

222 | BOB DEASY

and then you're off again like a madman. What before was random blue is now textured sky. It takes forever, but you know you're finished when you have a coherent story that makes sense at every entry point. For that reason I was a much better investigator for having been an undercover cop: I understood the court process, could spot the weaknesses in a case, recognized the probable defence strategies in dismantling it and didn't have the learning curve or make the rookie errors that would cost the Crown prosecutor convictions. And whenever a case led me back into my subterranean element, all I had to do was let a little bit of the old me out, and doors opened right up. So it was a new life, but it fit like a glove.

The CIB had fifteen to twenty detective inspectors at any one time. When a call came in, you would travel to the crime scene and assemble your investigative team, make sure they had everything they needed, attend the post-mortem and interview the victim's family, friends and any persons of interest. *CSI* aside, there are no overnight lab results or forensic tells you can brandish in front of the suspects. You're the prisoner of the slow drip of time, and it may be months before you know what you're looking at. On the upside, forensics is a very close-knit community, like the UC underground. The OPP is roughly divided into Uniform on one side and Services on the other—Drugs, Intelligence, Surveillance, Gaming and TSB, or technical support. So out of the OPP's approximately five-thousand person force, probably fifty (at most) work in Drugs and twice that in Intelligence, twenty in Gaming, fifteen do full-time Surveillance and then there's technical and other support staff. It adds up to a fairly small percentage of the total workforce—and I would have interacted with most of them at some point in my career. Since the cases are all at different stages it wasn't unusual for my caseload to stretch into double digits; when I retired I had dozens of cases open.

It's the perfect job because for the rank (and the salary) you're not balancing budgets and presenting spreadsheets at town council meetings—you're still doing police work. One of the earliest things I learned about homicide investigations is that people die for the stupidest reasons.

An early homicide case was a hermit north of Cobourg, halfway between Oshawa and Belleville. He lived in a cabin back in the woods, and lowlifes from town would find their way out there to smoke his dope and drink his beer. One day some drifter acquaintances of his—let's call them Bonnie and Clyde—got wind of this floating party and showed up there in the middle of summer. Their plan was for Bonnie to go in first, flirt with the guy, get him aroused, seduce him and then Clyde would discover them, become outraged and demand he give them his truck. Proving that drug logic often works better in the abstract, the hermit refused to part with his keys, and when the rhetoric escalated, Clyde levelled a shotgun at his chest and fired.

Their disposal of the evidence consisted of hiding the shotgun in some bushes and burying the body in the outdoor firepit, then taking off in the hermit's truck for the Alberta oilfields to make their fortune. But not before stopping at Bonnie's apartment first for her to dye her hair black so that no one would recognize her—I know this because the bathroom was covered in black hair dye. They drove as far as Orillia, where they stayed two weeks in a campground.

When I got to the cabin, the door was wide open, the truck was missing and the firepit was covered in a carpet of flies. (What looked like a rotten log turned out to be a thigh bone that the animals had chewed down to the cartilage.) I got the anthropology department at the University of Toronto to help exhume the body, thus revealing the shotgun wound, which with a little diligence gave us the shotgun. Some late-afternoon reconnaissance at the local tavern turned up a couple of regulars who, strangely, hadn't been seen for several weeks. I got approval to release their descriptions and the licence plate number of the stolen truck to the media, pulled their bank records and connected the dots of their credit card purchases. I sent the detective team to set up on the truck once we located it, and we had them in a matter of hours.

Once they were in custody I put them in separate cells with a UC in the cell between them who surreptitiously wrote down everything they said, the gist of which was this:

BONNIE: You shouldn't have killed that guy.
CLYDE: It was your idea.
BONNIE: But you're the one who shot him.
CLYDE: Well, you're the one who was blowing him.
BONNIE: You told me to so we could get his truck!

About twenty minutes of that was like a one-act play when it was read into the court record. Clyde pleaded out, and after two days of an increasingly comical trial, Bonnie did the same.

Penetang (short for Penetanguishene), north of Barrie on Georgian Bay, was an early example of the super jails that have replaced the old district jails. Central North Correctional Centre features a central repository and holding pen for everyone waiting to be assigned a space, all corralled together. A civilian, a little Asian guy, had been warehoused there for unpaid parking tickets—two weeks or $2,000 was a common sentence. All you've got to do is watch any episode of *Oz* to know that once you back down in prison they're going to use you as a feather duster, so this guy was no doubt already on edge. To keep himself occupied he played the board game Life with three other inmates at a table in the commons area. When he went to use the bathroom a big black guy took his place and wouldn't give it back when he asked. A hapless tourist oblivious to the codes that govern prison behaviour, the delinquent ticket-payer decided to make an issue out of it, and once the situation turned physical, against all odds he tore the big guy apart.

What no one bothered to tell him was that the big guy he'd just taken apart was a ranking gang member, bivouacked there between court appearances—King Louie, we'll call him—and now the prison grapevine was broadcasting this news to its captive audience quicker than Facebook. King Louie had to do something about it or else risk sacrificing his now-tenuous authority. So that night after lights out, he and two henchmen rolled into the guy's cell—each pod is locked down, but the cells within each aren't locked—and shanked him sixty or seventy times, just to make a point. When the guy didn't show up for roll call the next morning, the guards found him on the floor of his cell, which was covered floor to ceiling with blood. When the press got hold of the story, his epitaph became that for the sake of unpaid parking tickets, a young man in the prime of life suffered a brutal, painful death while trying to play the game of Life. The irony was lost on exactly no one.

When I got to the site, the first thing I discovered was that the super jail's vaunted surveillance video system had failed to work. We immediately put the place on lockdown. We also shut down the sewers, where they had traps under every sink and toilet, and quickly isolated bloody clothes, towels and the murder weapon. Other civilian inmates (i.e., non-career criminals who were there for minor violations) who had witnessed the afternoon's altercation corroborated the nature of the beef, and in turn we made sure they didn't have to spend another night in there with the lifers. Just as we were about to charge King Louie and his two minions, we got a call from the warden, who informed us that one of the minions was out at a court date in downtown Toronto, where his lawyer had just gotten him released. We knew the section of town he was most likely headed for, which just happened to be under the jurisdiction of one of my neighbours, a Toronto city detective. I got him on the phone and said, "Hey, it's Bob, your neighbour," and quickly explained the situation.

He said, "No problem" and hung up. Two hours later I got a call from Toronto police that they had the guy in custody. They had gone to the giant housing project he was from and started door-knocking until they found him.

He told them, "I've been released!"

The cop said, "Well, you are officially unreleased."

Lumpety-bumpety-bump right back to his bunk, which was still warm. We arrested him the next morning. Whenever you have three guys dead to rights, it's pretty likely one of them will flip, and we had everything wrapped up by close of business.

I also investigated several high-profile robberies that fell within my purview as major cases. One involved an Eastern European gang that targeted bank machines in big-box stores like Costco or Home Depot. They were ex-military types who were trained to stay completely still for nine or ten hours at a time. Two of them would enter the store during business hours and find a place to hide where they couldn't be detected. After the store closed and all the employees had left, a third member would cut the alarm outside. This automatically brought the police, as well as the store manager, who came and met them with the keys. Together they would do a walk-through of the store, where the two men still remained expertly hidden.

Invariably these huge warehouse-style stores have birds that nest in the rafters that can trigger motion detectors. When the police couldn't find anything, the incident was listed as a false alarm and everyone went back home. Then as soon as the coast was clear the two commandos came down out of the rafters and peeled the ATM open, usually with tools that were for sale in the store. The ATMs were usually bank affiliated and could have up to $80,000 in cash on hand. With the alarm dismantled they could literally blow the doors off the hinges and no one would know. They were working their way across the province when we finally caught up with them.

Along with their current homicide workload, virtually everybody at the CIB was assigned to some cold cases, revisiting homicides from the '60s and '70s. In these situations new technology might have finally caught up with available evidence. When we showed up in the jurisdiction where a cold-case crime had taken place, we had to negotiate with the local authorities over what sort of access and manpower they would provide us, unlike with contemporary cases. Municipal resources being what they are, the answer was most likely nothing and no one, and by the way, I'm afraid we're going to need that desk. So a large part of my time was spent building a team to meet the needs of each specific case, drawing liberally from both my network of resources and what I found there on the ground.

One such case involved a girl named Debbie Silverman who was abducted in Toronto in 1971 and later discovered buried in a shallow grave in Sunderland, north of the city. (Coincidentally, it was my friend George, who was with me in the Bike Squad, who had discovered the body on his very first day on the job in the OPP.) It took about a year, but two other detectives and I managed to narrow the persons of interest to a man who was residing in a psychiatric facility. The OPP ultimately decided there was no percentage in it and didn't want to spend the money, so they pulled the plug. It's one of just two cold cases I retired having failed to solve. The other one was more recent. On October 30, 1998, Jake Just, eighteen, took a shortcut through a swamp after partying on a hill in Midland and was never heard from again. I thought both the Silverman and the Just cases could have been solved, given the leads that existed and the suspects they'd narrowed it down to. I think all cases can be solved eventually, if you feed them the necessary money and time.

For the truly entrenched cases, the ones where they had somebody they liked for it but couldn't prove it in court, some forward-thinking detective inspectors came up with an ingenious technique that became known as "Mr. Big."

Evidence either convicts a suspect or it doesn't. If it doesn't—and you'll know pretty quickly—you have only a few Hail Marys at your disposal: confession, corroborated by some sort of holdback—crime scene details unreleased in the media that presumably only the perpetrator would know; an eyewitness who comes forward to testify; future evidence—either a break in the case, or a new category of forensic evidence that emerges, such as DNA. But with traditional policing, the half-life on having any of these breakthroughs is typically about six months. Mr. Big reinvigorates the possibility of a confession by incentivizing career criminals to give up their darkest secrets, freely and of their own volition, through the simple exploitation of the con man's greatest gift and closest ally: greed.

Here's how it works. When police have identified the most likely suspect in a murder investigation, but the evidence as it exists is not sufficient to convict, they will engineer an arbitrary meeting between the suspect and a low-level undercover officer through "happenstance." This can take any form, from a random meeting in a bar to a "meet cute" worthy of the most saccharine Hollywood romantic comedy. If you've got a wiretap up on his phone, sneak into his garage and puncture all four tires. When he calls a tow truck, have a UC standing by to show up in his place. Four flat tires is more than enough of an icebreaker to start a conversation: "Man, somebody must really not like you." From there it's a short leap to "I've got a buddy who owns a garage; he'll fix your tires for half price if you know where to score him a half-ounce of weed." (Any dues-paying criminal will still know where to score cheap weed.) Now it's nothing for the UC to roll by in a few days and say, "I'm off early, you want to smoke a joint?" Or, "This guy I helped out of a jam gave me four tickets to an all-you-can-eat buffet. You want to come along?"

If he rarely leaves the house, maybe we cut his power. When he calls hydro service on his cellphone, we send our man out, and in no time it's coffee to a sandwich to "Let's get a beer" to wherever you want to take it. Maybe it's a hobby, a mutual interest or a common emblem of a shared past.

Detectives have already interviewed the suspect thirty times, so they know everything about him; it's right there in the banker's box along with the rest of his file.

However they manage it, once the UC has established a rapport with the target, he raises the possibility of some quick cash. "You want to make a thousand bucks? You don't have to do anything; you just need to watch my car while I'm inside. I've got to take care of some business, and I don't want anyone fucking with it while I'm gone." The UC picks him up at midnight and comes back to the car in a hurry, leaving the distinct impression he's just committed a robbery, then peels off a thousand bucks, free and clear.

The next night, it's, "Can you do me a favour? I'm not supposed to farm this out, but I'm strapped. I need you to meet this broad at a train station tonight, she'll give you a package, just take it to the corner of Yonge and Bloor and a guy will ask you for it. Take you half an hour. Pays fifteen hundred."

A week later, it's, "These guys I know are going to boost a semi-truck out on the 401 tonight. The driver's in on it. They just need someone to drive an extra car." Pretty soon they're calling you.

Every job escalates; each one pays more money. Over three months or so, the story emerges that the UC's buddies are all part of a well-established crime syndicate. They pull all manner of jobs—anything that can be contained in a single location, limited to a small number of participants and not involve violence. With each new job the target is given more responsibility, and afterwards his performance is singled out for praise. At no time does he meet the head of the crew.

This is Mr. Big, the leader of the gang and a figure frequently described in terms of both fear and awe. The kicker is that everyone the target meets, from the garage mechanic to the girl at the subway station to the guy driving the tractor-trailer rig—everyone in this criminal universe that's been spun into existence around him—is a cop. It is manufactured reality, scripted in beats but improvised in real time, like some state-sponsored version of *The Truman Show*.

Eventually Mr. Big requests a meeting. That's where I came in.

So far I've been in the shadows, no more than a veiled presence. We meet in an expensive suite at some elegant hotel like the Four Seasons and I begin an intensive grilling: part executive job interview, part EST session or intensive psychotherapy. His work has been exemplary; he's held his mud, shown his mettle. He's exactly what we're looking for. I go over our long-term plans, break down the kind of scores we routinely pull down. His end could easily be worth six figures. Maybe there's a permanent place for him in our crew. There's just one thing.

If we take him on, we're the ones with the most to lose. He knows who we are and how to find us; if he gets popped, all he has to do is give us up and he can skate free. We're carrying all the exposure. What we need is insurance, something he's done that's so major, the repercussions of which are so incriminating, that he would never risk us telling anyone by selling us out. We would each hold something over the other's head in a kind of mutually assured destruction. It keeps everybody honest.

Like any criminal put on the spot he'll have some glib answer. He cheated on his taxes. As a kid he had some brushes with the law. He's pulled a few jobs here and there. He spends a lot of time on Internet porn, buys and uses drugs, has availed himself of prostitutes in his time. Each of those I brush away as inconsequential. I look at the situation and do whatever I can, for as long as it takes, for the real confession to spill out. It might take mere minutes, it might take hours. Whatever happens, I do everything to make sure that I've done nothing to force his hand. It's over when he gives himself up.

The first one I did was while I was still undercover with the Russians, so I had all my expensive toys to establish character—the Armani suit, the Rolex, the brand-new Mercedes roadster. The meeting lasted six hours, but I've done ones that went as long as a dozen hours.

A man who lived north of Guelph had allegedly strangled his common-law wife. I was purposely kept in the dark about the particulars, so I had to improvise during our talk. He confessed to a few scattered crimes, things he thought I'd like to hear—none of it passed muster. When he finally broached the murder, I told him I had lawyers and detectives on my payroll, and maybe I could bury the records of the crime—but he had to give me all the details.

I told him, "You may think you're a master criminal, but I guarantee you nobody's that smart. I can send in a cleanup crew and you won't have to worry about this ever again."

His first pass at a confession was both vague and clinical—told in the passive tense, taking no responsibility, as if sanitizing it for polite company. So I would take him back through it: What happened then? What did you do after that? In the room next door the cover team and detectives watched us on surveillance camera in a makeshift command post, including the inspector currently working the case, Donny Birrell. (I'd first encountered Don back in Geraldton and he'd been my boss in the Kenora drug unit.) Periodically I'd get a call on my cellphone, with Donny stage-managing my questions or steering me in a particular direction, since I was flying blind—calls I pretended were high-level business that couldn't wait. We worked out the rules of engagement beforehand with the Crown attorney, the prosecutor who would try the case: I knew it was a homicide, but not whether the victim was a man or a woman, the means of death, the motive, where it occurred or anything else about it. And once I was finished, his story would need to be corroborated by details that had been kept from the public, to ensure he wasn't just repeating what he'd read in the papers. At one point he volunteered that he'd burned his clothes in a nearby gravel pit, and I asked him where he got the gasoline. He said he stole it from a neighbour's garden shed, and we were able to confirm a police report that the neighbour had filed about the theft. We went to the quarry and located remnants of his clothing where he said it would be—which was done in real time as I was talking to the suspect.

Meanwhile, I welcomed him into the fold and told him that two of the other crew members would drive him home. They were waiting outside and were therefore not privy to what the cover team already knew, so when they came up I told them he "got the job," which we'd agreed beforehand would be my signal that he had confessed. They were wired for the ride home, which allowed them to make sure he hadn't lied just to get through the audition with me. Two days later the cops picked him up at his apartment.

Another one I did later became an episode of the A&E series *Cold Case Files*. Twenty years ago a woman named Marie Lorraine Dupe was murdered in Sydney, Nova Scotia, while working her very first all-night shift at the Big Ben's convenience store during one of the worst snowstorms on record. Patrons found her in a pool of blood behind the counter; she had been stabbed more than forty times. It was one of the most brutal murders in Nova Scotia's history, and because there was a notable lack of logical perpetrators, suspicion fell on her husband, whom she had recently married, and who had disapproved of her taking the job. When I got involved a dozen years later, the local townsfolk had all but tried, convicted and executed him for the crime. He'd lost his job, his friends and his life was in ruins. As the song says, "No one's interested in something you didn't do."

A forward-thinking Sydney policeman had thought to save cigarette butts recovered at the scene of the crime, even though the use of DNA evidence was still in its infancy and there was no such thing as a national database. A dozen years later, DNA from the butts got a hit on a domestic assault case in Mississauga, west of Toronto, which meant that the Peel Regional Police would inherit it as a cold case. But when two Sydney officers flew to Mississauga to follow up, they couldn't get the time of day from the Peel police and returned home without so much as a courtesy meeting.

A guy I'd worked with in Kingston Drugs nicknamed Caper happened to be from Sydney, and his parents lived next door to the investigating officer. When the officer complained that they had gotten no reception at Peel police, Caper's parents told him to call their son at the OPP. He did, and Caper in turn called Bowmaster, another one of our Kingston crew who was now a Homicide inspector. And Bowmaster called me.

The suspect's name was Gordon Strowbridge. Working with the Cape Breton Regional Police, the OPP set up an operation whereby we picked him up on a warrant for stolen goods and had a UC befriend him on the way to jail. After they were released, the UC drew Strowbridge into a series of fake car thefts, until it was time for him to make my acquaintance. I arranged to meet him at the penthouse suite of the Harbour Castle, a nice hotel on the waterfront in downtown Toronto. This was maybe my fourth Mr. Big case, so the surveillance team set up in the room next door knew how they were likely to go. They had a betting pool going on how long it would take me to crack him. Strowbridge walked into the suite, this massive room overlooking the harbour, and as his ass was hitting the couch, he said, "Yeah, I killed a girl." They played the tape probably a hundred times in court, and at one point you can see me stare right into the camera as if I'm asking, What the fuck do you want me to do now? He had spent enough time with the other UCs who'd set up the Mr. Big scenario that he understood the score. He gave me his whole confession, including that he had thrown the murder weapon in a snowbank, a detail that had been withheld from the public, which sealed it for us.

Since he'd confessed so fast, I had to keep the interview going for appearances. In the course of him laying out his CV, he told me he'd spent time living in Kingston and had even been staying in a boarding house where seven-year-old Sharon Reynolds had died under suspicious circumstances, her body found stuffed beneath the stairs. I pushed him hard on it, but the more he talked about it, the less likely it seemed: unlike the Sydney murder, which he spoke freely about and made no effort to deny, he was very emotional about the death of the child—crying and really shaken up. He also had a solid alibi. But for the Dupe murder it took him all of thirty seconds to confess—and nobody from the surveillance team won the pot.

After Strowbridge had been sentenced to life in prison I received special commendation from the mayor of Sydney and the citizens of Nova Scotia, and through the police chief, the husband sent me a message thanking me for giving him his life back. That's the single most gratifying thing that's happened to me as a policeman.

There were endless variations on Mr. Big. My next one we referred to as Mrs. Big, a.k.a. the Black Widow of Pembroke. We set her up with a lot of deliveries on trains—diamonds, jewellery, it didn't matter: take the train from A to B, get off at the other end and give this to the guy in the grey sweater. As payment we gave her a credit card with a $500 limit and let her bang up purchases. (This was after the Eaton Centre project, and like Levi Strauss, the credit card companies were more than happy to hook us up.) Eventually we gave her cards with a $15,000 limit and had her bring us the balance in cash.

We were convinced that she had killed her husband by crushing horse tranquilizers in his food. She was in her forties or fifties and her husband was much older. She had recently waltzed him into the bank to get his bank accounts and property signed over, and she had a sweet tooth for well-appointed pensioners—she had buried four previous husbands. You'd think that looks would have been essential to her job performance, but she was, let's say, less than attractive—marks all over her body from getting poked with ten-foot poles. But she threw herself into her work, I'll give her that. As soon as one job was over she'd be on the phone again, ready for the next thing, sexually propositioning the UC, recommending new scams. She thought she was the bomb.

After about six hours of her interview she volunteered the detail about the horse tranquilizer, which no one knew outside of us. I mean, thanks, Agatha Christie. Who would even think of that? She told me her friend was a secretary in a veterinarian's office so she got eleven hundred doses of some particularly strong chemical and just sprinkled a little on his cornflakes every morning. She said he was vomiting and defecating everywhere and she had to clean it all up; it was the worst six weeks of her life.

There was also a version of Mr. Big called Mr. Dead. It was predicated on something called a dying declaration, which is a term in law that refers to an exception to the hearsay rule: hearsay is legally admissible at trial if the statement is made by someone who is dying, as a form of deathbed confession. It's more common than you think. Mr. Dead, also known as Dying Donny Davidson in homage to a fellow UC, exploits this loophole by dressing up a UC as a dying criminal, then convincing the target that in exchange for money paid to his next of kin, he would be willing to take on the burden of the crime in question and confess to authorities. In order for his claims to appear authentic he'll need unknown details of the crime, which the target is then hopefully persuaded to provide. A variation on this technique is where the UC confesses to the murder, and then Mr. Big confronts the target and says he couldn't have committed the murder because he was somewhere else on the same date, and the police know it. Mr. Big then demands to know who really committed the murder, in order to deflect a police inquiry.

A Mr. Dead play was actually behind the conviction and subsequent death of a famous murderer named Barry Manion, who molested and strangled a twelve-year-old girl in 1970 in Kirkland Lake, near the Quebec border. Robo and Scotty were involved tangentially in that one. Almost forty years later, in the course of a Mr. Dead sting, a UC revealed to Manion that he was dying and willing to take the rap for the murder. But the bond between them had grown so strong by then that Manion told him, "I can't do that to you," and instead turned himself in to police. He subsequently led police to the wooded area where he had buried the body, and three months after pleading guilty he hanged himself in his cell.

I had a 100 percent conviction rate on the Mr. Big cases I did, and my buddies and I have all done our share of them. Robo did one where he bonded with the target at a lake-side cottage, spending days at a time alone with him, where they had plenty of opportunity to share and recount their pasts in detail (or presumably for the target to chop him up into little pieces). Took him a year to get the confession. He's also done a lot of cases where they put him in a prison cell for twenty-four or thirty-six hours with a target—handcuffed in the paddy wagon, waiting in the bullpen and then shacked up in a holding cell together. One I remember, this guy with a wild look in his eyes told him a whole intricate story about how he'd been smoking meth and got into a fistfight, and this guy Angel kept pissing him off, so he hammered him into a wall. It was only after Robo got back and filed his notes that he found out Angel was an infant, and the guy was up on charges for the aggravated assault of a baby.

Scotty did one where the target entered a contest to win an all-expenses-paid trip to go salmon fishing and he won, and Scotty was another winner on the trip with him. He also played the Mr. Big character on a 2006 murder where the target, Steven Hill of Haileybury on Lake Timiskaming, had allegedly killed a young man, Perry Reaume, in the back of a van. The body was never found, though the skull was. The primary UC had gotten in with Hill and was over at his house, staring out the window at the backyard, when he saw a clump of something coming up through the ground.

"What's that?" he asked.

"Oh, I thought I got rid of that," said Hill. "That's Perry." He freely recounted the whole murder in detail.

The UC said, "You idiot! You can't just leave stuff like that lying around! You call yourself a criminal. Let me get rid of it for you." The UC dug up the skeletal remains, put them in a bag and drove straight to police headquarters.

On a related note, I'm not sure this technically qualifies as a Mr. Big, but after Robo did the Satan's Choice in Project Dismantle, a guy who'd gotten ensnared in some related credit card fraud—let's call him Gary—tracked him down and said he'd been having an affair with a lawyer's wife and mother of three. The couple was going through a divorce, and the lawyer had successfully hidden all his money. Since she knew Gary was affiliated with bikers, she demanded he get some members of the Satan's Choice to kill the husband or else she was going to tell the police that Gary had raped her. He was worried that his bail would be revoked, and Robo was the only cop he knew to go to. Robo told him to give the woman his number. When the call came, he and a UC buddy wired themselves up and went and met her. A rocket, he described her as—tall, blond, eminently available. She was willing to seal the deal with the two of them right there in the back of the van. Robo set up a second meeting to give her a chance to reconsider; instead, she showed up with Christmas card photos, $3,000 cash and some tips on how they might go about clipping him. She was sent away for four or five years. It would have been longer, but she'd never had so much as a speeding ticket before.

And then there's Smitty.

A woman named Judith Thibault disappeared a dozen years ago from the Intercity Mall in Thunder Bay. They found her car parked there, but she had vanished. Four years later some guys doing surveyor work near Wolf River found her body rolled up in a carpet. Her common-law husband, Michael Kelly, was always a person of interest, but the local police could never get any traction. Wiretap, polygraph, even showing him the autopsy photos in all their vivid glory—nothing. By then he was up working on the Alberta pipeline. I helped brainstorm the bump—how we were going to meet this guy. Kelly had reportedly been obsessed with his wife's pension investments and rental property, so we knew that greed was our ally. As Smitty says, "Greed or lust—pick one."

Smitty posed as a private investigator working for one of the big banks. They backed the plan up with credentials, investigative records, a website—they had to fool lawyers on this one. The play was that Thibault had an insurance policy that had never paid out, and Smitty was performing due diligence before they abandoned the claim. Kelly had been living in New Brunswick before moving west, so Smitty went up there first and created a whole paper trail by knocking on doors and exhausting leads, most of which got back to Kelly up in Alberta. When Smitty finally called him, claiming he had a modest insurance claim to pay out, Kelly said, "Send it to my lawyer," and hung up on him. Smitty managed to convince him that he had to sign for it in person and set out for Beaverlodge, Alberta, about three hundred kilometres from Edmonton, near the British Columbia border. It might as well have been the Casablanca of the North, since everyone up there was a fugitive of some stripe. After some small talk Smitty got his signature on a release and paid him $500. He also offered to run a check to make sure there were no more outstanding dividends.

A couple of weeks later Smitty returned and said there was a second unpaid insurance policy—this one for $800,000—which the company had stopped payment on because of suspicious circumstances. It's like a civil action: even if no criminal charges have been filed the company can still deny the claim on suspicious grounds and shift the burden of proof onto the beneficiary. Smitty came armed with letters from the police, internal memos from the bank and consultations with a lawyer. After laying out the case he informed Kelly that there might be one solution—if they could shift the blame onto another suspect, the bank might relent. Smitty knew a guy with terminal cancer who might be willing to admit to the murder—for a price, to be paid to his selfless eighteen-year-old niece and caretaker. He also had a guy inside the bank who could grease the skids, but he didn't come cheap. And, of course, Smitty himself would need a little taste for all his trouble. He could orchestrate all of the above but would need every detail of the crime, public and suppressed, in order to spin a convincing tale.

"The devil's in the details," Smitty said.

They finally met with the cancer shill, Donny (as in Dying Donny Davidson), in a hotel room in Toronto, since Kelly refused to travel back to Thunder Bay. He showed up at the meeting with Thibault's ring to offer as proof. But the further down that road they went, the more nervous Kelly got, until finally he said, "I'm not going to do it."

Smitty went ballistic, said the money's already spent, started kicking the furniture and raging around the hotel room.

Eventually Kelly said, "All right, you want to know who killed her? I killed her."

"I don't care whether you killed her or not," Smitty said. "You're a lucky bastard. I envy you. But the less I know, the better. Don't tell me anything else. Save it and tell it to Donny. If it works, fine, and if it doesn't, Donny's gonna die anyway."

To celebrate, Kelly said, "I ought to get me one of those Chinese whores."

Smitty said, "This is Toronto, man. You don't even have to go out; you just pick up the phone and call them."

About forty minutes later there was a knock on the door, and an Asian prostitute entered and prepared to demonstrate her wares. On the surveillance tape you can see Smitty looking at the camera as if to say, We'll be seeing this again in court.

Once they were co-conspirators Kelly gave up the details of the murder to Donny and went down for life.

Smitty's also the guy who once did a takedown of all the street-level humps on a particular drug project by offering them a job promising easy money for little work. Here was his pitch:

"Be ready tomorrow morning at eight with a yellow safety helmet and a reflective vest. I'm coming by in the bus. Gotta be yellow; can't be white. I wear white—you wear yellow. Pack a lunch because we're going to be gone all day. We're conducting an ecological survey. Can you hold a pole? Good, you're in. Don't make us late."

One guy even asked if they could pick him up at his girlfriend's house. Instead of sending out five-man teams to crash through doors, Smitty just drove a short bus all over town and picked up twenty of these guys, then pulled over to the side of the road to let the cover team board and put them all in handcuffs. For a lot of them it was the first honest job they'd signed up for in their entire life.

We've suggested having a think tank that does nothing but brainstorm Mr. Big scenarios, but just like with everything, management wants to know who will pay for it.

Technically the Mr. Big technique—and I hate that name, by the way; it sounds arrogant and self-satisfied, even if it's used ironically—applies to only a small percentage of murder cases. They have to be cold-case homicides; they have to have a single prominent suspect, with evidence not strong enough to convict; and the suspect has to still be involved in, or at least susceptible to, criminal enterprise. In my time working as a homicide investigator I was never tempted to mount a Mr. Big investigation because I never had to; there was always a new avenue of investigation, and eventually it led to an explanation of the preponderance of the evidence. All the Mr. Bigs I worked on were undercover jobs that I did on the side.

Mr. Bigs are legal under Canadian law, since the government empowered us to commit pretend crimes under special designation. But since the days when we perfected it, the Mr. Big technique and its many offshoots have largely fallen out of favour. Public perception is that the alleged perpetrators are often bullied into confessions, or seduced or entrapped. Those convicted by it have claimed they feared for their lives, and there have been books and documentaries chronicling these alleged abuses. I don't take exception to many of the specifics, but I believe that in *every* case where such criticism is credible, the fault lies not with the technique but in the way it was utilized.

I lay this problematic outcome almost exclusively at the feet of the RCMP. They have routinely violated key tenets of the strategy, mainly the firewall that exists between the investigators and Mr. Big himself, to the point that they have sabotaged their mission and established bogus case law. The Mr. Big character cannot know the details of the crime, or he's just a sidewalk barker trying to steer a mark into a Yonge Street peeler bar. If you know where you're going, you just have to trick the target into coming along with you. That's sophistry. Smitty translates the method into the line "When I kill someone, I like to use a hammer—how about you?" Leading a witness to evidence is like leading a horse to water: it gets you nothing. There's an old saying in the drug op world that goes like this: "If you see a guy with a gram of hash and you want to turn him into a trafficker, offer him a thousand bucks for it." Now he's sold you $1,000 worth of hash. Except that your ploy will effortlessly unravel once they put you under oath, because the system has checks and balances built into it to protect against exactly this sort of knavishness and trickery. It's a specious claim and a ridiculous tactic, and it deserves the derision it would engender. Success is judged by when you get to the truth, not when you rack up a conviction. Not to mention, there's no challenge in that. What's the thrill of getting a conviction based on counterfeit proof? It's like cheating at cards. I've spent my career building a reputation in the service of Queen and country. To risk that on false evidence or fake convictions—essentially on entrapment—is suicidal.

Conversely, if the target produces intricate, detailed knowledge of the crime or crime scene that were unknown to the public, he's guilty. Period. He can't be intimidated into producing that information. He can't be tricked into it. The claims that details can be fed to him beforehand—even without my knowledge as interrogator—don't hold up, because I would ask my questions from every possible angle. Describe the scene. What's to your left? To your right? What's she wearing? Turn around—what do you see? What's the weather like? Describe how you got there. What do you see on the street? And on and on. You can repeat notable facts by rote, but there's no way to manufacture the minutiae of an experience. All of which can be compared to the case file and photographic record after the fact. All I knew going into one of these Mr. Big scenes was that there had been a homicide, and that if I kept pushing, there would be a payoff at the end. I wouldn't even know the gender of the victim. There's no way for us to entrap anyone when we don't know where to lay the trap.

Even if we have a confession, a confession alone is worthless. People walk into police stations and confess to crimes they didn't commit every day. It's one of the banes of our existence as investigators. If we were just interested in clearing homicides, we could take them at their word and all knock off early for the day. That's not the gig. The gig is to elicit a confession that sticks, meaning one that is corroborated by thorough and robust investigation. With Strowbridge, he told me he threw the knife in a snowbank. He said he smoked cigarettes inside the store, and in fact his DNA was on the butts. He walked me up and down the aisles, pointing out where the blood was, and we could verify it with photographs. The Black Widow of Pembroke identified the kind of horse tranquilizer, and it was there in toxic traces. She told us where she got it, and we could subpoena the vet. The guy who burned his clothes told us where he stole the gas. There's no way to luck into that kind of detail. And if there's a question, the whole thing's on videotape—which is usually played in court.

These are not hardcore master criminals, by and large. Such people are largely a Hollywood fiction. Ninety-nine percent of homicide victims are killed by someone they know, and more often than not it's some kind of stupid accident or emotional power surge that the perps a second or two later wish they could have rethought. And they're usually glad to get it off their chest, even if they think they're going to win a prize.

At the end of the day I'm prepared to walk away from a case if I haven't made it. The reason the Mr. Big cases have such a high rate of success is not because cops force them through or nail them shut—it's because they rarely go into them without a pretty clear idea that they've got the right guy. They're too complex and expensive to mount otherwise. They're a way to further an investigation when the chain of evidence has hit a wall. But combine that evidence with a voluntary, informed confession, and it doesn't look so stark. That's what a Mr. Big gives you. And if somebody violates that, threatens the target, puts a gun to his or her head and tells the person to confess, that's not an institutional flaw; that's just a bad cop—somebody who's seen one too many movies. The sooner those yahoos are out of service, the better for everybody.

THE END OF THE ROAD

Be careful what you wish for.

I was a cop for twenty-three years; almost fifteen years I spent undercover—from the day when I first knocked on a safe-house door and a looming vampire biker scared the bejesus out of me, to the day the FBI put me on a flight out of Miami and the Russians toppled while I was airborne. I got out in 2006, when much of what I had learned and many of the skills I had painstakingly acquired suddenly seemed beside the point and behind the times. In the span of two decades policing had changed considerably. I could see the bureaucracy mounting almost hourly, like a backyard creek in an afternoon rain. Actuarial martinets who learned about policing from television dramas routinely erected Olympic-sized hurdles in our way for the joy of seeing us scale them, or more likely falling short. Disillusionment settled across everything like a fine powder. At least that's how it seemed.

By that point the original Flying Squad and its similar iterations had been neutered by cautionary regulations, many of them policies that my friends and I had inspired. I always thought we made it much more difficult for the next generation of undercover guys coming up, because every time we did a project, the bad guys would receive another free playbook special delivery.

But the mentality had changed as well. Union provisions were now designed to keep officers out of harm's way. Technology—advances in DNA profiling and forensic science—rose to fill the gap. Equal-opportunity crime, the kind that offered a platform for charmers like me, was being replaced by ethnic or religious affiliations that were impossible to infiltrate the old-fashioned way. The cowboy attitude once considered a virtue by my generation was now considered reckless, if not kamikaze. What we once did and how we used to do it could scarcely be believed by the people doing it later. They looked on us with a mixture of pity and wonder, like three-legged dogs with our hide burned off in patches, running the internal arithmetic on how we could still be alive. It was not difficult to see that I was staring into a world where my skill set would soon become a liability.

And so I got out. I had a friend who owned a stone quarry, and it seemed like a way to be outdoors, to work with my hands and steer clear of the shadows. No more subterfuge, synchronicity, sixth sense or nine lives; what could be more unambiguous than blocks of stone dug straight from the earth? So I bought it. When I told my boss in Homicide, he said, "Fuck, that's excellent. I wish I was going with you." My close friends knew it was coming, but when word got out, to a man my co-workers who were my age or older said some version of "I wish I had the balls to do what you're doing."

I had achieved my goals in the OPP, on my own terms, without compromise. The next two ranks above me were purely political, full of budget crunching and administrative backstopping, things that held zero appeal for me. I know my limitations, and I am not an office beast. I need a steering wheel in front of me and a problem at the end of the road. So instead of cashing out, buying an RV and moving to Mexico like a lot of guys, I froze my pension on the advice of a financial planner so that I could avoid the penalty.

After a time I discovered that I missed the work, even if I could do without the bureaucracy, so I joined the Office of the Fire Marshal as a fire investigator. It's identical to my life in Homicide, except that I don't have the bureaucracy to deal with, and I don't have to assemble a team, draft project plans or search for money. I just do it myself. We're mandated by the province to investigate every fire where there is death, serious injury or suspicious circumstances. There's a good reason every fire marshal is an ex-policeman.

Truth be told, I was part of a dying breed. After the years in Homicide and a lifetime undercover, the road had caught up with me. I was a veteran of local wars, and all my comrades now are counting down the calendar to join me in the pale Valhalla of civilian life. We were starting to see second-generation criminals—the sons of the men we had stalked and put away, now following the same well-worn path as their fathers. This was where I came in. It was time to go.

"I'm gonna cry at my retirement," says Smitty. "And I'll use words like 'service' and 'honour.' But let's face it, we're fucking dinosaurs.

"We're a bit of an anomaly," he adds, "in that of the four of us in particular, although there's been lots of hiccups and battle scars, glitches in our personalities that are a result of that, we've basically come out of it unscathed. I'm not crazy. I've got zero desire to go out and blow my fucking head off. I've got a great life, and I've got life experiences that precious few can touch."

When I became a cop, I thought I was going to be the guy on the white horse. I feel that we were the best at what we did, above the law in certain ways, but in none of the ways you'd think. It wasn't the entitlement or arrogance you'd imagine, or at least that wasn't the engine. It was being the best, pushing ourselves out past the recommended performance-stress levels, to see how far we could get and still make it back. Not for the adrenalin rush, but to push ourselves into blue sky. As often as not, the people we worked for and with saw us as wild or uncivilized, the devil's platoon gone native. We were outcasts as much as anything, the guys who performed a necessary service but couldn't help bringing back some of the taint that rubbed off on us. Unlike our randy neighbour to the south, where outlaws are celebrated and mythologized, here in

Canada we feel a quiet disdain for the criminal or miscreant. A media gag in the courtroom keeps criminals out of our consciousness, at least some of the time. A leak to the press could mean a mistrial. At best Uncle Charlies hold a distanced fascination, like lions in the zoo. We may have been heroes, in some kind of existential sense, but we could never take credit, get our picture in the paper, do our victory lap. We were ghosts, if anything. That unremitting, pressurized existence was like a disease you couldn't turn off. It kept us apart from our wives, our families, the mitigating aspects of civilization and often the simple pleasures that make life bearable. We internalized everything, packed it down like powder and hoped that when it blew, the people around us would be standing clear.

What we did instead was invest in each other. It forged us into a makeshift family, one that took pride in solving our own problems. There's a BBC series from a decade ago called *Births, Marriages and Deaths* about three old friends who share the hallmarks of their lives. That about sums it up. We were agents of the law who spent all our time trying to become the best criminals we could be. I built my alter ego, the professional identity I wore in lieu of body armour, out of bits and pieces of the mentors and role models I encountered along the way. For outsiders looking in, especially other cops, I think that made them either envious or resentful. They either wanted what we had, or else they attributed something unwholesome to it. That's what made us into such a tight-knit, bonded group. These are the only guys in my entire life who were always there for me, no matter the consequences.

Here's what I've learned: if you think you're going to win the "war on drugs," eradicate a scourge, save a generation, retire a social behaviour, you're misguided. Even your wildest successes will only roll up a distribution network or incapacitate an executive leadership of some permanent criminal enterprise. We solve crimes, but we'll never solve crime. It's no less a quantity than infinity. The best we can do is manage crime—discourage it on occasion, dismantle its mechanism briefly, maybe dissuade its practice in isolated cases. Everyone wants us to be social workers, but just as often we're human garbagemen.

I take pride in the work I did. I never had a rabbi—in police culture, that older functionary who keeps you out of trouble and saves your ass when you need it. And I never got deep in the shit, which is rare for a guy with my pedigree. There were some guys who got further up the food chain because they perfected the politics or found a niche, and I don't begrudge them that. And there were complete buffoons who took credit for others' labour, including mine. The guys in the trenches know who they are, and they've withheld their respect accordingly. I'm confident I have the respect of the men I've worked with.

I didn't get into policing because of the money. When I started out I didn't even know how much I was making. I've had friends tell me that if I worked half as hard for myself as I did for the OPP I'd be a rich man today. But there's not one of us who couldn't wait to get back to work or out on the road. All those tales that still fly around the Garage Mahal, wherever its truest state may be, that's what guided them.

I wouldn't trade it for the world.

ACKNOWLEDGEMENTS

Bob Deasy would like to acknowledge:

Smitt
Scott
Robo
Jed
Dino
Yank
Buck
Pipes
YaYa
The Amigos
Commonwealth Crusader

Johnny Three Beers

Dougy Two Beers

Gigg

Carson

Baz

Caper

Nam

Al

Kid

George

Caffer

Hoss

Ernie

Brownie

Buck

Jack

Grogger

Ace

Cankles

Smokin' Joe

Pistol

Tromper

Chippy

Fluf

Gordo (RIP)

Ab

Buff (RIP)

Chelsea

Cory

Bucket

Joey Montana

Jacob

Rosiak

Forehead

Corky

Pope

Glennie

L.W.

Bleeker Ridge

Booger

Neutron

Spinner

Doc

Billy Burke

Donny Wilson

Wink

Mr. Champignon Ed

Bow

Big Jack

Sliver (RIP)

Cookie

Team B

Clarkey

Earl

L.V.

Ty

Spike
Terry
Whitey
Taber
L.A. Rich
Point Ideal

Mark Ebner dedicates his end of this collaboration to his Canadian expat father, Herbert Ebner, M.D. He also wishes to thank: Pamela Murray; Joel Gotler; Brian Lipson; Jerry Kalajian; Paul Cullum; Jenny Pool; Jerry Langton; Lisa Derrick; Lisa Ullmann; Rebecca Weinstein; Mandy Stadtmiller; Stacey Grenrock Woods; Joshua Leonard, Mary Ebner and the Enright family.

INDEX

BOB DEASY spent over two decades deep undercover for the Ontario Provincial Police. He recently retired as a Detective Inspector and resides north of Toronto.

MARK EBNER is an award-winning journalist and *New York Times* bestselling author. His latest collaboration, *We Have Your Husband* (Berkley True Crime, 2011), was recently adapted for a popular Lifetime Network movie of the same title.